A Portrait of Words
Divinely Speaking

A Portrait of Words

Divinely Speaking

Ornitha Danielle

A Portrait of Words Divinely Speaking Copyright © 2015 Ornitha Danielle

This book is a work of the author's creativity. Ideas, themes, examples, places, events, and incidents are the product of the poet, writer, novelist, and author's very own unique creativity and are used artistically. Any resemblances are merely coincidental.

Any and all locations, situations or circumstances in reality are disclosed in this book to give a feeling of real life situations and issues that will bring clarity to the story that is being shared, and conveyed through words.

Printed in the United States of America.

Library of Congress Control Number: 2015900168

Published By: So Fyh Diva Publishing Ink Inc., & Ornitha Danielle
E-mail addresses: danielle_taylor2006@yahoo.com
info@ornithadanielle.info
editor@sofyhmagazineonline.biz
sofyhdivapublishing@gmail.com
Website: http://www.divinelyspeaking.com
Website: http://www.sofyhmagazineonline.com
Website: http://www.sofyhbookreviews.com
Website: http://www.ornithadanielle.info
Photo on the front of the book cover © Lee Taylor of So Fyh Photography
Book Cover: Ornitha Danielle and So Fyh Diva Publishing Ink Inc.,
Editors/Proofreaders: So Fyh Diva Publishing Ink Inc.
Content Editor: Lee Taylor
Proofreaders: Lee Taylor, Tara Woodley, Vena Darling, and Arcinko Smith

CONTENTS

Dedication

I dedicate this book to the love of my life, my lifetime partner, my soul mate, Rodney (Lee) Taylor, Sr. Thank you so very much for all the love and support you've shown me once again in my literary projects and assignments. Your pushing has helped me to keep going. I am hopeful this is just the beginning. You'll always have my love for all eternity. Without you in my life, none of this would be possible. From my heart, I could write you a letter all day and every day. It is such a great pleasure to be alongside of you. I find joy in being with you, to have your ear to hear my ideas and thoughts. I know at times that I can be a real pain (I had to add that. Lol). I am so thankful that God placed you in my life to love, help, and encourage me along this journey.

Your Wife,
Ornitha Danielle

Dear Reader,

I want to personally thank you again for sowing into the creative work that God has given me to share with you. Please understand that I am not just taking this lightly. Thanks for blessing me to be able to bless you. This is a literary ministry and I am grateful to be able to share these parables, poems, and deep thoughts with you as God has given me. With every word that is within the pages of this book may it bring to life the situations and realities that many believers of Christ face in this dark world that we all live in, but with a hope for a brighter tomorrow. Abba Father surely has a way of showing us things about who we are in him and what he wants us to do. Each and every poem will indeed impact lives, and address some of things that are happening right at our own front and back doors. Ask yourself these questions: What do we do? How can we help one another do better?

We can pretend that there is nothing happening, but really who are we fooling? Why do we make excuses as to why we do not want to get involved? We cannot continue to allow the enemy full control and access over family, friends, and our lives. We must stop choosing to keep silent. It is my hope that from these pages you are awakened with a deeper understanding of what lies here and there and in between. I am asking that you allow the mere words from this poetry book to spark love and compassion to make a difference, and that your heart is changed to touch other lives.

Let us be about Kingdom Building and lead others to Christ. Let us allow Him to finish the work that he started in us before the beginning of this foundation. As you begin to read, you may find that you may know someone that has or is dealing with some of the things that are written here.

Ornitha Danielle

Acknowledgements

First and foremost, I must give thanks to **GOD** for creating me, and for blessing me with the ability to write, create, and express myself through words. I thank Him for his son **JESUS CHRIST!** Without **HIM**, I wouldn't be possible, nor would you be reading these very words.

I would like to thank my husband, Rodney (Lee) Taylor, who has been such an inspiration to me. I appreciate all that you've done to help me with this process. I know that you've given a lot of yourself to help make this second book be as great as the first. Thanks so much for the sacrifices that you've made, not getting as much sleep, and listening to me talk about all these ideas. I know that I can go on and on about this.

I would also like to thank my children, Antonio (TJ), Dy'Neshia (Neshia), and Lil' Rodney (Stank), for being some really amazing children. Watching you grow into young adults is something that I'm especially proud of. Every time I write, I think about how precious life is and how time flies by, so I said that to say, never allow something that's a dream of yours get away from you, no matter how hard you think it is or how far away it is. If you can dream it, then you can do. Whatever you put your mind to, it can be DONE! I know that one day you will be doing some very amazing things, so go out there and make your mark in this world. Be the great woman of God, and the great men of God that I have raised each of you to be. Be the leaders that I know you can be.

To my grandson, Austen (My Scuttabug). I know one day you'll pick this book up, read it, and know that I love you very much. No matter what's been done or said you are loved. Know that I have been here and have always been. I love you so much!

To my girls…Vena, Traci, Tara, and Arcinko, you ladies have been some positive influences in my life. Some of you I met early on in my life, others later, but that doesn't matter because you all have made an impact on me. We only get so many friends that come in and out of our lives. Each one of you have been in my life for over ten years. I'm so blessed to have friends like you. I love you.

To my online family and friends. Thank you again for your love and support. I really appreciate you for getting the word out about my books, and all that I am doing. It really does mean a lot. Although we can't pick and choose our natural families, God gives us what we need, when we need it. I am very blessed and thankful to have such a strong online supportive family! ☺

To a very special woman of God, my mentor and spiritual mother, Apostle Theresa Harvard-Johnson, of *Voice of Christ Literary Ministries International*. I truly thank this woman for the activation in literary ministry and for her obedience to the Father in heaven for her assignment. Your words have been radiant in my life! I thank you for the words of life that have been spoken into the dead and dry place in my writing. I never knew how important it was for me as a scribe to write these books as God has given me. I know it was truly God that connected us in every way, just from my assignment in the Kingdom of Heaven. I'm a Scribe to the **KING**! I'm enjoying the keys to this ministry that I have been blessed and chosen to walk in. It is my job to complete all that has been entrusted to me as his servant. I know that words couldn't ever express my appreciation. I salute you! I have been awakened since the time God sent me to *Voice of Christ Literary Ministries International*. My life hasn't been the same. I see myself as **THE KING SEES HIS BELOVED DAUGHTER!** Words could never express what you have done in my life. I cherish the true friendship, love, and support that you give me just when I have needed it. Proverbs 27:17 says that *as iron sharpens irons, so one person sharpens another*. What a true woman of God you are. I now understand and know what that means. I thank God for your transparency and for allowing me to peek into your life to see what it's all about. I once thought I knew what it was, but now I see what it is to be a true woman of God! I bless you.

I would like to thank my spiritual mother, Apostle Denise Chase, and *Know Your Worth Ministries* for helping and encouraging me during my transition into where I have come at this place in my life.

Thank you to all the newspapers, magazines, radio stations, bloggers, and interviewers for allowing me to share my story and my journey with each one of you. Thank you for the much needed support.

Special thanks to The Mtenzi Award, Ma'9 Mustardseeds, and The Stone Awards. It is an honor to be recognized for what God has placed within me. I'm completely humbled by it. Special thanks to the Founder, Stanley Campbell, and his organization, for even creating such an event that pays tribute to the arts and those that are finding a place at HOM! (House of Mtenzi).

To all of my readers, it has been more than a great pleasure once again to share yet another book with you. I know this has been a long road, but it has finally come, well almost come, to an end. I know many of you have been wondering what I would come up with this time. Well, this has been a work within itself. My prayer is for those that hold and read the messages that are being conveyed within the content of this poetry collection, to allow your mind and ears to understand what is being said by the way of the Holy Spirit.

These words are a creative expression of the spirit of God, and not meant to ordinarily entertain. This is a literary ministry to inform, educate, and bring awareness and clarity to the many things that I have had to face, and a testament of how God brought me out. It is to expose the powers of darkness in the earth. This literary ministry is combing real life struggles that so many in the world are trying to overcome. However, with the help of God, all things are possible.

Just because we are Believers in Christ, that does not make us off limits to encountering life's problems. There will be many obstacles to face, but we have the authority to speak to that issue and believe that God will remove it!

I pray as you read this that it ministers to you in such a way that you'll never be the same, in Jesus name! Father, in your son Jesus' precious name, I pray that the words, examples, and details that have been imparted into me, your servant, touch the very spirit of the one that reads that which you placed in me.

May it be a blessing to them.

Father, I ask you to remove every hindering spirit that comes to block the messages in this work of ministry that have been entrusted to my hands. God, I ask you to pour back into the person that is reading this right now. Father, I ask you to allow the words to uplift, uproot, build, tear down, deliver, and set free your people. Lord, make every crooked path straight, in the mighty name of Jesus!

Introduction of Poetry

As I sit here thinking about how I should introduce you to the elements of my writing, my mind is racing about the things that I could say. However, the best thing for me to do is to allow the Holy Spirit to speak through the pages of this book. There are things that you may not understand, but my prayer is that in time He will reveal it to you. Sometimes, it can become very difficult for me to find the words to express or explain what it is that I write. This can be a complicated task for even me, but I trust God to do just that, which is to guide. These words not only came from me, but they have been a part of me as well. Some of them have been a place of just me having conversations with Yah (God) concerning my life, and how he leads, comforts, and loves me through my pen. I pray that the FIRE within YOU will be IGNITED! Ignited to grab your pen and notebook to write down your own thoughts that only you can hear.

John 8:36 KJV If the Son therefore shall make you free, ye shall be free indeed.

Lord I Praise and Worship YOU!

If I couldn't say another word,
I'll wave my hands and give you total praise.
My hands and my feet belong to you,
I worship you in spirit and truth.
It takes all of me to give you total praise
My soul my heart belongs to you.
Lord, you are the reason why I breathe and with my voice I sing,
With my hands I worship, with my feet I dance.
I use all of me to praise and glorify you.
If you never do another thing for me, you've done enough.
Lord, you heal my body and mend my heart from all the pain.
Father, I know you know my thoughts and my heart,
My heart belongs to you.
I love you, I love you, you are the reason I praise you.
My worship, my hands, my feet belong to you, so I worship you.
There are no trees and rocks going to out praise me, I'm here to
worship you.
If it is the last thing I do, I praise you.
I want to see your peace when you come back for your Bride.
With every tear that I've cried,
my life has been made complete when you rescued me.
With the anointing of the Holy Spirit,
my praise and worship is not in vain.
I worship, I cry out to YOU.
As you minister to me, I listen to your voice
and I understand that you are molding me.
Lord, I praise and worship you.

For That I Am Wonderfully Made

Looking at this image in the mirror, the reflection I see is me
Wondering what could be changed to make things be as I see.
Noticing the inner beauty and poise
that overtakes the essence of what can be
The warmth of the sunshine that rests upon my face,
Seeing the path where tears once had left a trace.
A smile beneath all the hurt, trials, and heartache
has made who I am while running this race.

For That I Am Wonderfully Made

The deep scars of the past
have shown me that trouble don't always last,
When my back is up against the wall
I realize that when I kneel to pray,
all my giants must fall.
Walking through the doors
that have been opened up for me to go through,
I know that it's you.
Thanking God because of the words
HE has spoken to me,
and assuring me that I am free.

For That I Am Wonderfully Made

The moon and the sun shares the sky along with stars
No matter how far or low,
there is time when we will reap what we sow.
Learning to live again,
and the truth in love will find you in the end
Here are my hands to fight
for I am stronger with the power of God on the inside.

I truly love with all my heart, not even thinking about my raging
adversaries and their fiery darts

For That I Am Wonderfully Made

As I position myself to have a talk with God,
I sit still and listen
as He speaks to my heart.
No questions are asked
about the instructions that were given,
I know that I have been commissioned
And I am on a mission/

For That I Am Wonderfully Made

I have an assignment that I must complete
Reaching for the scroll I know that
I must write the vision and make it plain
I am an inspired scribe a vessel preordained,
To do a great work and it will not be in vain.
What I write comes from a place of contentment
Not a place of despair

For That I Am Wonderfully Made

I am always praying and not preying,
I am diligent seeking and not slacking,
I am trusting and mediating on
THE WORD OF GOD
I am listening to the voice of the Lord
I am obeying what HE has spoken.

For That I Am Wonderfully Made

I am from a royal priesthood,
I am awaiting my kingdom reward.

I am victorious,
I am standing on the promises and fainting not

For That I Am Wonderfully Made

I am willing to go where He sends me,
I am a child of God
I am a faithful servant
I am what God says I am
AND
For That I Am Wonderfully Made

The Comforter

Down on my knees
with my hands outstretched to the heavens,
My heart is heavy and my mind is weary.
The tears that fill my eyes
cause my vision to become blurry,
Crying out for this nation
And the people of God.
The Lord is tugging on my heart
To feel for those in the dark.
One, two, and three,
In Christ Jesus we are free.
The joy of the Lord is my strength,
A presence of love
lands on the shoulder like a dove.
The angels rejoice as shackles fall
from those that are bound.
Now, we as saints can wear our heavenly crown.
Reading our daily word,
Praying for direction and guidance,
Obeying what the Spirit of the Lord has said.
Build up and come boldly before the throne of Grace,
Only the strong will win this race.
Allow others to be ALL that the Lord has called them to be,
We no longer are going beyond the hidden veil,
It has been has been removed
To worship at his feet.
He is The Comforter
He is all we ever need.

My God

I didn't understand what road I was traveling,
I didn't understand the heartache that was unraveling.
To stand in the midst of my trials and tribulations,
God began to reveal His sweetest revelation.
Standing in place to speak as bold as I should,
My character and personality quirks always misunderstood.
My unique qualities, my wildest curiosity
God's hand rest upon my head,
My prayers cause my worst enemies pure dread.
So, I stand here with my arms outstretched with the anointing
From God's appointing.
Tears I cry, as I look to the heavens on high.
Oh, Lord, thou art Holy, Holy, and Holy
As I approach the throne room boldly.
How great are **YOU,**
To shield and protect me through and through.
No matter what tests may come,
I know that the victory is already won.
Kneeling at your feet,
I know that my enemies I will beat.
For your love is unconditional,
I worship and I adore **YOU** eternally.
Your name shall remain upon my lips,
Your word has been written in my heart
Because you are My God.
You are Alpha and Omega.

A Heart to Heart with God

I did my very best, and I gave my **ALL**
But my heart is still hurting for the stress of this mess.
I prayed the prayer that God's will be done,
I cried my last tear because the victory I've won.
Thinking that I could have done more to make things different,
to let others know what is to come.
As I was told, God answers me,
I have seen what's up ahead.
So, you just wait and see what I show thee.
Lord, I have tried to stay on the right path,
God responds…
"There's a time when failure will come
from not obeying my words of direction.
Let me show you," says the Lord.
"My word is sharper than any two-edged sword.
Keep your mouth closed from this point on end
for they shall know the wages of sin.
Don't fret my child,
they will see what was told to them,
by my servant that I sent."
I replied...
"My, my, my, how I cry for the nation and the people of God,
the rich, the poor, the sick, the heartbroken and weary.
God asks....
"Whose side will you pick;
the choice is yours."
I replied...
You are the only one I will follow,
I trust only you,
and my love for you is like no other."
God says...
"Come with me my child,

I have something I need to you see,
do not worry about what others may think or say,
THIS IS MY WILL FOR YOUR LIFE.
I take His hand and follow,
no questions asked.
I do as I'm told,
Because I know that God
holds my future in the palms of His hands.
My eyes have seen,
And what my ears have heard,
destruction, anger, hurt, and
Families are being ripped apart.
Fathers and sons fighting,
Mothers and daughters,
Brothers and sisters killing,
Hurting each other,
Honestly, all of this has grieved my heart.
I fall to my knees, I cry out,
Oh, Father what can we do to change this?
What can I do to make them see?
My tears roll down my face like warm honey.
I cried out in a plea, Lord, Lord help us,
have mercy on our souls,
The government is suffering,
education and jobs are falling,
so much of this has happened
because of disobedience,
ignoring the Righteous calling:
Not understanding at first what I was shown,
it became very clear, time is closer than ever before
stand up for what is right and watch and see
HOW GOD WILL GET THE GLORY IN OUR SIGHT.
Father, why has my life been in such turmoil,
So much heartache and pain?
God said, "I chose you.
I know the road has been hard,

but I was with you through everything.
I've seen what you've endured,
I've heard everything."
I said, "I'm not sure why you picked me."
God replied, "My child,
what you endured was not meant to kill, hurt, or destroy you,
Only to build you and make you stronger.
And return you to me,
I HAVE REDEFINED YOU FOR A PURPOSE."
"Oh, Lord, I have done all that," I cried.
I want to share, tell, and encourage your people.
I think I have missed it somewhere and somehow.
I have begged and pleaded, and cried out on their behalf.
What do I do?"
"My child, everything is where it should be,
and so are you.
Keep standing and believing in me.
I know you trust me with your heart,
everything that you have laid at my feet
will come to pass, hold on.
I have recorded every tear that you've cried,
I know your heart; that is why
I choose you,
I hear your prayers.

I Can Only Live For Today

The moment that I opened my eyes this morning, I began to thank God for allowing me to see another day. He told me what happened yesterday is gone, and today is going to be a brighter one with many benefits.

As I pray and thank HIM for all the things HE has done in my life, and even what HE is going to do, all I can do is cry out to HIM. My life is nothing without HIM. The Word says I can do ALL things through HIM that strengthens me. I trust and believe that whatever I'm about to face, HE will be there with me.

I used to fear what others thought and how they would not hear what I had to say. This day the Lord has made. This day I will abide in Him. This day is not given to the swift, but the strong.
I can only live for today. No matter what it looks like, no matter what others think, no matter how I feel or how much I want to give up, **I can only live for today.**

Yesterday is gone. Today is now. Tomorrow is the future. Tomorrow isn't promised to me. **I Can Only Live For Today.** I see the writing has been on the wall for a long time. I must now learn that I cannot change what happens. I can only go through in order for me to get to the next chapter. I never pretend to be more than I am.

My heart is true. I am a friend. I am not a fighter. I have the love of MY GOD on the inside. My heart will not allow me to mistreat others, nor will it allow me not to help.

I Can Only Live For Today

Randomly Thinking

Wondering if there was such a place where people could truly be happy and free. Thinking of a special moment in time, as everything drifts into slow motion. Hourglass shows time slowly passing by. Watching the sunrise and the birds glide across the sky, randomly thinking, *why can't I?*

An emotional connection can be the skepticism one feels as it approaches them. Very apprehensive about the desire to feel, left in a trance. Despised by such a feeling. No one can ever tell what to conclude. Chained by the pass doesn't mean that a person can't move forward. It is who they are.

Past disappointments, let downs, and people not being there for you, it's okay. Learning to overcome, that will be the challenge, but it can be done. Loving one's self is the key, because no one can be *you* better than *you*. Hold your head up high and never look back. Walk into your destination.

I do what needs to be done, knowing that I have finally won.

Surprisingly

There was a point and a space in time during my life, when I felt like crying, always wondering if my tears would ever stop coming. I looked at my situation as the harder it became for me to get to the next step or phase in my journey.

I never fit into any group or category. I was always doing me alone, and became pretty good at doing just that. But for some odd or crazy reason, I allowed others to try and create a new me, instead of me just being me. I became bitter, stressed out, and grew angry with them.

I dare never to allow anyone or anything again to have that kind of power over me, unless you have walked 3,000,000 plus something miles in my life.

I have learned that it is okay to say *no*, and one shouldn't feel bad for doing so. I even thought that what I was doing was never good enough for what others thought I should be doing. I walked around for years, hoping, praying, and wishing that people would just leave me alone.

Before you judge a thing or even try to figure out how to change it, get the facts first. I have really learned how to live and not allow life to outlive me. Never judge a book by its cover. I am a masterpiece within! I am happy and all smiles. I have walked many miles.

Just Saying

I've always wondered why so many people
have the hardest time letting go of their past.
Looking at the present is just temporary
because it will be gone tomorrow.
Some never look forward to the future,
too afraid of being happy,
but comfortable being empty!
Love is what we make it,
so many times people fake it.
It is just a matter of time
before someone realizes what has been done.
So many people put all their trust into people and they get hurt,
You're in control of your feelings, thoughts, and emotions.
Never allow anyone to control you
Be true to yourself and honest with others.
You may lose friends along the way,
Thinking back on how individuals see you,
ask yourself these questions.
Do they really care about me?
Do they respect what I do?
Should I put my feelings aside to be their friend?
I'm just saying, stay true to you.
Love who you are and what you will become.

God's Sheep

We can live inside a plastic bubble and think that we're too good to receive correction and wisdom from others. **THAT'S PRIDE!** I speak the truth and expose the enemy and his agents of deception.

Age doesn't suffice that one has gotten all the knowledge there is to really know. There's still much room for growth. It's almost heartbreaking when you put yourself in Jesus' place, and realize all that He endured. My heart broke to know that I had treated Him this way by being disobedient to His Word and not listening to His voice. The Bible tells us that His sheep know His voice, and a stranger they will not follow. "Hello Danielle!" The light bulb went off many times. I'm like, *Okay, Danielle, you have to get it together. The Lord is talking, so you need to move.* God called me His sheep!

We should live a godly life before others, and have a teachable spirit. A dear friend of mine told me, 'I'm a greedy person in the spirit. I want everything God has for me and that you can give.' I laughed at that, but I get it now. There are many that have traveled some of the very roads that you may be traveling and can keep you from getting off course. If you'd just listen, the Bible tells us that the old women will teach the young. I can appreciate these nuggets! Clearly, we can show love and learn how to correct in love.

When we come to a place of full maturity, understanding, and knowledge, we will be all right. Somehow, people tend to get so puffed up in pride that they miss their own blessings. They allow the flesh, and sometimes the enemy, to distance them every single time.

I was reading the story of the Apostle Paul *aka* Saul. I thank God for this clarity. This man was knowledgeable in the word of God, but lacked the love and compassion for the people of God! He operated out of the gift of what was taught to him until one day he had an encounter with Jesus Christ! Now with what I know from the Word, combined with the anointing that God placed upon him (What a combination), he became much more than he could imagine. This man was spiritually blinded, which manifested naturally.

Sometimes God will use drastic measures to get our attention. God uses these drastic measures, turns them around, and gets the glory that is due Him. Every single time we think that we've arrived to that point in life where we believe we know it **ALL,** there is more to know about GOD and we discover something new. One thing is certain, God is **ALL-KNOWING!**

If you know me, and have come to me personally and spiritually, you know that I have the **BIGGEST HEART** in the world for **GOD'S PEOPLE.** I will help, encourage, and pray if I am asked to.

We should learn how to become transparent about what we've done in our lives and during our walk with the Lord. I have truly learned some powerful things along this journey. I am so grateful to the **God-fearing** men and women that He has placed in my midst who freely pour themselves into my life. I pray that I am that same blessing to others.

I asked one of my friends a question the other day just to see if she really listens to me (it wasn't some trick question). I asked her if she knew who my favorite woman of the Bible was. She was like, "Dani, now you know I know that. It's Hannah." I was so tickled because she was right! I love Hannah's story. There are many other women in the Bible that, through their pain, were pushed into their purpose.

Hannah, in my mind, had an awesome prayer life. She had everything naturally, but she wanted something more than anything, and the only way she knew to get it was to go before God. I can appreciate that on so many levels. I can truly say that the Lord remembers each of our prayers.

I want to see God's people restored, and on fire for Him like never before, in other words, **IGNITED**! One of the places I dare never to be is out of the presence of God. I leave you with this: When you take care of the things and the people of God that He has placed in your life, know that it's unto the Lord.

May God's pure love overtake you as you read this. *If ye abide in me, and my words abide in you, ye shall ask what ye will, and it shall be done unto you.* God will not go against your will.

I pray that you receive Him into your heart today. Let us not be like those that Christ speaks to in the book of Matthew 23. Let's be about our Father's business and not our own. Let's do just what Jesus did when He walked the earth. **AMEN**! I bless you and love you with the love of the Lord! I know where my help comes from.

Lord, I ask you to pour greatly back into those vessels that have poured into my life by way of this book even now, just as I'm praying for you. In Jesus name, **AMEN**!

I love hearing the word of God. My love for God is so awesome. God's word has been so rooted in my heart; I can't get enough! The Lord said, "Let go of it. I'm trying to position you for much greater! Walk into the new, but you must leave **ALL OF THE OLD BEHIND**! You can't carry it with you." Many in the Bible had to leave the old behind in order to receive their blessings. Yes, sometimes it does hurt, because we are comfortable. But we

17

can't stay in a place of comfort. It's time to mount up like eagles and spread our wings. It's time to soar to new heights, new hope, new joy, and new strength. "Come deeper," said the Lord. Will you come?

I serve a God that is strong and mighty! What a friend I have in Jesus! Breaking through with **VICTORY**! Sounding the **TRUMPETS**! Sometimes it's the signs that God reveals to us right before it happens. God is wonderful.

BLESSINGS BELOVED. God's days are blessed. Be ye blessed and favored of the Lord thy God! May the blessings of God be refreshing as you go about your day. Remember to pray for one another and love one another.

Walk in love. Treat others as you want to be treated. They are the seeds you sow and plant in this season. God's grace is with you!
I am throwing my hands up in the air and giving God my total praise. I truly thank Him for preparing me for this journey. It does soften the blow. I am a conqueror, I praise you, God. I shed tears of joy! Ain't nobody mad but the devil.

It is sad and heartbreaking to see so many in the "Entertainment Industry" tossed aside after being used like yesterday's leftovers! This is happening in the Christian and secular areas. I know this isn't the life that God had for them. Lord help! The degrading, the manipulation, the abuse (mental and physical), sex, drugs, the spirit of compromise, are all an outrage.

I'm praying for these individuals. Mark 8:36 (KJV) says, *For what shall it profit a man if he shall gain the whole world, and lose his own soul?* Proverbs 10:22 (KJV), tells us, *The blessing of the LORD, it maketh rich, and he addeth no sorrow with it. "The Lord is my portion,"* says my soul, *"therefore I will hope in him."* (Lamentations 3:24, ESV)

Lord, we need your help. People are losing their lives for nothing. When God is for you, then who can be against you.
With the authority given to you by the Father, you can send the enemy fleeing from you like 75 going north. The enemy should be terrified of you coming into the room. Allow God to increase in your life so people will see the God in you.

Speaking Truth

DIVINELY SPEAKING. People often reject what they don't understand or believe. Just because it doesn't make sense to you, don't discount it. Be ready for God to reveal Himself as you seek Him. Even in the midst of it all, God gets the glory!

GOD IS SO GOOD! GOD'S BLESSED DAYS TO YOU BELOVED! SHALOM TO YOU AND YOUR HOUSE. THANK GOD FOR FAVOR AND LOVE!

Falling in love with Jesus is the best thing I've ever done. Don't be afraid, but trust and believe **GOD** to supply just what you need. Look at it like this - what you need is already there. You just need to step out on Faith.

Thank you God for waking me up this morning. I'm going to get my mind on you even more. I hear you loud and clear. When Father calls us to do something for the Kingdom we should obey. Do not worry about what will happen to the next person. Jesus made that very clear as I was reading recently about Apostle Peter. He asked Peter if he loved him. That was so profound. It had such an impact on me that I mediated on it. It's still in my spirit as I write this book.

You've been charged to be obedient to God, too. Don't worry about the next person. Do what you've been asked to do. Your answer should be, *Yes, Lord* each time. One day at a time sweet Jesus!

I thank you for all that you're doing in the lives of your people. I thank you for this day! There's a war going on, a battle for the souls of the people of God. Wake up and look at the many signs around you. The word of God changes not, God is raising up an army that is ready, willing, and not ashamed!

We must be careful of what we allow into our eyes and our ear gates. If it's not building us up spiritually, we need to reevaluate it. It should be about Kingdom Building and Living as Christ intended us to live. Follow the examples Christ left behind.

We have been purchased with a price. We are more than overcomers. Open your eyes and see yourself as He sees you. God loves you and desires to have a relationship with you. It is time to stop *doing* church and become the *living* church.

May God reign in your heart. Allow Him to have access to every area of your life. He will meet you right where you are. I know that He will.

The Choice Is Yours

There are many decisions that you must make when it comes to how you want to live your life. Would you rather live a life full of regrets? Think about it for a moment…Okay, times up! Now look around you, look at the news, the changes in the weather, medical insurance, and the cost of food, which is skyrocketing.
The point is with everything that goes on in this world, and around us, it will all soon come to an end. Where will you spend eternity? It's like this; no matter how, who, what, when, or why they did or didn't, or whether it was or wasn't fair, God is the only one that can repair whatever it is. So, forgive, let go, and move forward in your purpose and destiny.

When you begin to seek God for answers, you will start to uncover the many hidden treasures about you and your purpose. Then there's no more asking, "Why am I here?" Every question that you have is an answer to this question. Nothing in the Kingdom of Heaven should ever cause you to feel less qualified to fulfill the work that God has called you to do. Everyone's ministry or calling isn't the same. It is the same spirit but it operates differently.

What you did in your past doesn't have to keep you away from what God has planned for your life. Think about it like this. The Apostle Paul was notoriously known as Saul before his conversion. See what I mean? Dig deeper into the Word and see what the word of God has to say concerning you. **THE BIBLE HAS ALREADY BEEN WRITTEN!** My God! Here is something to think about. At the end of the day is what you've done pleasing to **GOD**?

LET'S BE MINDFUL AND HELP BUILD UP THE KINGDOM OF GOD. One thing is for sure, the enemy, very sadly, is building his Kingdom. Come on now, the Bible says we perish for lack of knowledge (Hosea 4:6), so why die before your time (Ecclesiastes 7:17), instead study to show thyself approved (2 Timothy 2:15). God wants all of **YOU,** not part.

Although we live in this world, we can't be part of it...(Romans 12:2) Don't copy the behavior and customs of this world, but let God transform you into a new person by changing the way you think. Then you will learn to know God's will for your life, which is good, pleasing, and perfect. **"MANY ARE CALLED, BUT FEW ARE CHOSEN!"** God is calling you out of darkness. Will you surrender and answer Him? **PEOPLE, WE NEED TO GET IT TOGETHER. IT IS TIME TO STOP PLAYING WITH GOD!**

Whatever you're facing on today, trust and believe that God has already worked it out for you. So, wait and watch God move. Look to Him, and to what lies in front of you. God wants to give you the desires of your heart. He is worthy to be praised.

GOD IS NOT PLEASED AT WHAT HE IS SEEING! LORD, HELP US TO FORGIVE! REPENT! REPENT! HAVE MERCY!

I have been in church pretty much **ALL MY LIFE** and have been led to believe so many things that are untrue. Now that I am in a place where God has started really opening up the scriptures to me like never before, I am feeling great! I have always been a cheerful giver and done so freely, never once questioning it.
There's a reason that I just shared that. It was because I want you to know that you still have time today to open up your heart and **GIVE IT TO GOD!** Be cheerful and allow God into your life today.

Being Mindful

I have had, at times, less than someone else, but I still gave to others that were far less fortunate than me. I never want anyone to think I'm coming off puffed up, arrogant, or thinking I'm all that and a bag of chips. I'm just sick and tired of so many wolves in sheep clothing using the Word of God and Jesus as a big business I'm tired. Do y'all hear me? It is just sad and it's a shame that these wolves are deceiving so many.

The Bible tells us how we are supposed to treat others, and love them. Don't get me wrong, every single time I see a child or a family on the street living under the overpasses, behind dumpsters, and alleys, and the very next person that tells me it's because they didn't prepare better for life, I will scream. How dare you. I am tired of these wolves with the wrong motives! I'm not bashing anyone, but what I am saying is that we really need to wake up and read the Word of God. It's very important to our spiritual growth. Our Bibles are indeed portable and travel with us. We can give to the less fortunate. We need to wake up.

People come in our lives for a reason, to get us to the next level. I'm walking with my head held up high in front of my enemies. No matter what bills or health issues I have, I am going to keep on pressing towards the mark. Peace, love, and blessings.

Surrender your brokenness to the Lord, and say 'YES' to the invitation to draw closer to Him. Trust God to mend your broken soul. Confess your faults and sins to Him. Tell God you are willing to let go and do things His way and not your own. He is waiting for you with open arms.

Food For Thought

I know that we **ALL** fall short of God's glory daily. So, if there are some things that are still under the rug, or deep in your heart, please let it go and **NAIL IT TO THE CROSS**! If you're still holding things, how can you hear from God or be effective in ministry?

This is something I haven't yet understood. I know that God is the only one that can change people. So, why do we try so hard to change people instead of allowing God to be God?

I'm singing and crying tears of joy! When I cried out and asked God for an answer, it manifested right before me. I know God's time isn't my time; it is God's will and I'm obeying Him. If you do not want to keep going in circles or repeating the same test over and over again, then whenever God says something you need to **LISTEN**! Sometimes we have to be still, wait, and listen to God.

Okay, I'm throwing my hands up in the air and saying, Lord this is your battle to fight. I am faithfully giving thanks. Rise and shine. Give God the Glory! Be thankful for such a wonderful day in the Lord!

Lord, I'm so ready. I feel you shifting the atmosphere. I'm following your lead. Whatever you want to do in my life, I'm surrendering my all. I Love You. My God. Only You, Wonderful Jesus!

Urgency In My Spirit

My God! Help your people! I believe that as people of God, we really need to stop playing and get close to Him like never before, because what is about to hit the world is going to have people confused, afraid, bewildered, and so much more. I urge you to get your houses in order today. I pray that you will take heed to what I'm saying. He's soon to return. Are you ready?

GOD, PLEASE HAVE MERCY UPON YOUR PEOPLE IN THIS HOUR. KEEP WATCHING AND PRAYING.

At one point in time I used to believe that it was all about status. That was what I saw most of the time. If you didn't have something, or didn't run with a certain crowd, you pretty much had to fit in where you could get in. I never liked those kinds of odds! Thank God for the blood of the Lamb, Jesus Christ. It feels wonderful to be accepted in the Kingdom of Heaven. Not by the standards of this world, but by the love of **The One** who made it possible to enter.

Do yourself a huge favor. **LOVE AND WALK IN IT AS WELL!** Just because someone doesn't fit into your mode, they are still a child of God. I am forever thankful for my changed mindset. I'm not placing God in a box to limit His ability to move in my life. I'm not in a box because that limits the access that God needs to do what He must do so that **I FULFILL** the purpose and destiny that has been already written about me, His beloved daughter. Yes, that's ME!

Just thinking about my journey over a year ago, my view has changed in more ways than one. The scales of my eyes have been removed and the plugs from my ears have once again been removed. **TODAY,** remember to put on the **WHOLE AMOUR**

OF GOD! Do not leave home without it!
THANK GOD FOR FREEDOM IN HIM!

God let your will be done in me. I will speak what you say speak! Decrease me, your servant, so that you can increase even more in my life. I belong to you. I am in your hands.

The Expectations

Sometimes when there are really no words to express what is in your heart, the remedy is to pray. I normally don't share deep things unless God tells me to do so. Especially about what I see and hear in the spirit. Well, one morning, as I was in prayer, just talking to the Lord as I usually do, a heavy and deep sleepiness came over me. I was trying to fight it, but I said, "Okay, Lord, you win! I was in this place of expectation. Whatever it was I wanted to see it. As I'm walking, looking. and I mean I was really looking, there was this door. (As I am writing this and explaining what happened, my heart is so overjoyed). The door was huge, tall, and wide. It was suspended in midair! There was this awesome glowing light radiating from all around it. I was so excited about what was behind that door.

This is what happened next. My eyes opened, and I woke up. I said, "Lord, no. I am ready to see it. Please, I'm not afraid." Immediately, I went back into that dream just like that. The door opened very slowly. With my nosy self, I couldn't wait, so I got all on my toes trying to see. This was the brightest light I ever seen in my life. The funny thing though, I didn't even have to squint or put my hands in front of my face to keep the light from shinning into my eyes. I saw a figure standing in the door. I started shaking all over. Now, at this point, I don't believe I was asleep anymore. I felt my body in the natural, like I was having a seizure of some type. While I was shaking, I felt this warm light run through my body. I never opened the door. It opened up unto me. Blessings were on the other side of that door waiting to overtake me. Expect God to be on the other side of that door for you.

Expect a miracle! I wanted it and it happened for me. It will happen for you, too as you believe, trust, and receive it. There is no room for doubting! God did it! **AMEN!** God is waiting on you. There was this sense of peace that came over me as I was standing in the door. I pray that whatever you are standing in need of, you will receive it in Yeshua's (Jesus) name.

When I talk to God I know that he will give me an answer. Oftentimes, you just don't have the words to say. Even me, the mind scrambling, yes it's true, filtered with mixed feelings, I can express myself via my pen! The very first inscription of words that were written on my heart, was God's Word. To understand His love for me, to think of the many things I did wrong in His eyes can be overwhelming, yet My God still loves me. The many things I did right made him proud of me. There's not a day that goes by when I'm not reminded of how much I am loved by him. God is the head of my life, this very life that he gave me. Lord, take me higher and into deeper depths of where you want to take me. Many may never understand your struggle or why you do the things that you do.

Dying to the old things and disobedience can cause things that have been asked for in the midst of praying to be on a brief delay because of the wickedness of the heart. It is God who searches the heart, and not what's on the outside. You can extend your hands and heart to others, but it's up to them to receive it. God, keep searching the hearts of your people.

In this season the Lord is saying that true repentance, is coming forth. There is no more time for playing games. The false repentance has come to an end, bitterness in the heart is coming to an end. God is saying that masquerading around in masks and costumes, hiding and living two different lives, is coming to an end. He is saying he sees you even when you're trying to cover up. Come from behind the charade of things. The Lord is saying, "I'm calling you out." There is deliverance and healing that needs to take place for the mind, body, and soul. "I need you to hear my voice, listen to me," said the Lord. "Repentance is for you! I want to set you **FREE**! Deny yourself. I have need of you."

29

Cultivating a Diamond in the Rough

Building the self-esteem of young teenage girls can be a challenging entity within itself, while destroying it is a lot easier. After looking at what society deems to be the latest movement on how a woman should look, act, think, and feel, it has become apparent that no one really has a clue. Society has become way off course here.

For one, God did not create each of us to be the size 4 which they consider to be the perfect size (at 98 pounds, fully clothed and soaking wet, standing 5 foot 9 inches in height). This false ideal starts our young women down the road of eating disorders and self-hatred because they are not up to what mainstream thinks they should be. Little do they know that these young women are "Diamonds in the Rough."

If we were to take a close look at how the diamond is created, many processes must take place before it can be a diamond. A jeweler places his glasses on to look deep into the diamond for the qualities that it has to have before it will become that perfect setting for a ring, earrings, watch, or necklace. It goes through extreme pressure and temperatures before it will even be considered. God is the same way.

He is the perfect jeweler. He knows what he wants us to have. God created us as he wanted us to be. We are blueprints, not carbon copies fresh off the assembly lines. There is no one diamond that is the same, just like a snowflake. Even though some twins and triplets may resemble each other, they are different.

We should encourage our young women to know that they are

beautiful. Teach them not to be ashamed of their full lips, voluptuous hips, and their natural hair. Tell them that they should be proud to know that they have been wonderfully made in the image of God.

Beauty can be purchased at a price, but at what price, one may ask. Recently, I saw pictures of Lil' Kim. It wasn't a pretty sight at all! She'd really messed herself up. She paid the price for beauty like so many others have who were not comfortable in their own skin. Too many times we've been looked over because of our bodies. Every single African woman is worth more than just her looks.

We need to build up our women to be productive citizens, business owners, wives, teachers, and lawyers. Encourage our women that they can be anything that they want to be when they put their minds to it. The entertainment industry is placing so much emphasis on wanting to women to be a Barbie. And I'm thinking, why should we encourage our young women to become a plastic doll? Honestly, I have not really figured that one out yet.

On the contrary, our women are rocking like something serious these days. We're in the White House! Michelle Obama sets the example for young girls; if she can do it so can they. We're even astronauts, doctors, and authors too. Let us tell our daughters, nieces, cousins, aunts, and friends that they can be all they can be just like the Army!

We can teach and lead by example. Who is the first woman your daughter will see? You are! So why not show her how a woman should carry herself. We should speak life into the lives of today's young women and tomorrow's leaders. Let them know they are much more than beauty and body. Tell them they have BRAINS!

When we see our young women going down the wrong road, we

need to keep encouraging them and showing them the right roads they should take. Tell them that they are built to stand against the negativity that others speak over their lives. Tell them they can do **ALL** things through Christ Jesus (Philippians 4:13). Encourage them to dream big and live life to the best of the abilities that God has given them.

Tell them it's okay to be comfortable in their own skin, and that they don't have to accept anything less than what is perfect in life. Tell them they have the ability to accomplish everything in life that's in the will of God. Tell them they have the right to be who God created them to be, and God makes no mistakes on how he created them. Tell them they are unique, gifted, and designed with a purpose. Society & media can be so cruel to the young woman. They tend to take her self-esteem away by saying, she's only good to be a baby momma, the other woman, and even worse, calling her a female dog? Really? There's enough wrong going on in this world, along with the negativity the media depicts.

Society and the media tells us the tighter the clothes, the more cleavage a woman shows makes her a dime piece. Come on now, really? There are some great things that have finally happened for us. After many years, we have an African American Princess that was created by Disney, even though it was a fantasy. Overall, it is important to realize that we have a face and voice in this world. We can be anything we want to be. The sky is the limit.

Family First

Many things can increase unity within the family. One of the most important things is prayer in the family unit. There is this old saying, "A family that prays together stays together."

Keeping a clear line of communication open will also maintain a healthy dialog between one another. Being honest about each other's' feelings, desires, hopes, and dreams can be effective. Keep outsiders or people on the outside looking in at bay. What goes on in your house should stay in your house.

Spending quality time together playing games, watching movies, going on a family vacation, are some ways to increase the bond of the family unit. Allow members of the family to be themselves and understand that each of us are made the way God wanted us to be. Do not overstep certain boundaries that will cause a breakdown in the family.

Each family member should support, encourage, and love one another unconditionally, no matter what. At the end of the day, we can pick our friends, but not our family.

I can remember, as a child, when my vision of the perfect family was the Cosbys of *The Cosby Show*." The father, Heathcliff Huxtable, was the perfect father. He was a doctor and a family man. Heathcliff was the support system for the family emotionally, physically, and financially.

In today's society, quite often the father isn't present in the family unit. If we were to look at how the people of the Bible lived as a family, we would see that family should be precious to everyone. Although The Huxtable's are a fictional family, one would hope and believe that somewhere down the line that this can really happen. Let's even look at the wife, Claire Huxtable. She was businesswoman, wife, and mother who still managed to be there for everyone, including her parents, just like her TV husband, Cliff.

Funny, I almost forgot. If we look at The Obama's we can see that a strong family unit does exist and they are quiet young. I'm not sure what goes on behind closed doors, but in public they are happy. Only one can imagine that The Obama's pray as a family, and individually, for their strength and for courage along the walk they are taking.

If we would spend less time fighting and more time loving one another, we can build the family that we all desire to have. If we had the opportunity to do so, naturally we would choose to be with a family that we have no business being in from the start. God gave us the families that we need and what He wanted us to have. Think about it like this, if it wasn't for the family you have, you might not be the person that you are today. We should thank God for the families we have. It's a blessing to even have a family. We can actually have the family we desire if we just invest the time and energy into them. ***HEALTHY RELATIONSHIPS!***

My Keys To Freedom

The definition of "Freedom" in our dictionary is *power or right to act, speak, or think as one wants without hindrance or restraint.*

The word freedom can have many meanings depending on how one interprets it. There is freedom of speech in the United States by the First Amendment to the United States Constitution and by other state constitutions and state and federal laws.

If we look at the unity of marriage, the official often says at the end of the ceremony, "Speak now or forever hold your peace." We have the right to give voice to what we think and how we act and speak on issues that concern us as a people. Many times freedom can be taken the wrong way.

The Bible tells us in the King James Version (John 8:32) *And ye shall know the truth, and the truth shall make you free.* John 8:36 states, *If the Son therefore shall make you free, ye shall be free indeed.* We have the freedom to worship where we want. We can live, work, and even shop in the stores we desire.

The Bible also tells us that God created man with freedom when he placed Adam and Eve in the Garden of Eden. They had freedom to do as they liked. However, with that there were rules that should have been followed. The only thing that was off limits to them was they were not to eat from a certain tree. Just like today, we have freedom to drive down the highway, but the laws of the land control us. We have this thing called a speed limit. If we break the law, we are punished. We are free to do as we like, but we have to obey and abide by the rules. That is with everything we do, unless we have our own companies. We make the rules and regulations for those that want to work for us.

Let's go back to the laws. How can a law say that we have the right to do certain things, but as we continue to read down to the fine print, as a woman they can try to take my rights away and dictate what I'm to do with my body. Really? Roe v. Wade in 1973, is a landmark decision by the United States of Supreme Court on the issue of abortion, the 14th Amendment. Yes, I know it is very controversial! We are still facing, today, our rights to have children, or even where we wish to live. But sometimes, in actuality, our freedom is only to a certain degree. Ask yourself these questions: Do I have freedom to do as I please? What will it really cost me to have the freedom that I want? Will my freedom cause me to gain or lose friends? Think about it. Yes, again someone else is telling you what to think, what to say, and how to feel. Therefore, are you really free to exercise the freedom you desire?

In Perfect Tune

My body knows not the emotional course that it will take, but it builds up a wall that won't shake. The keys play the perfect tune, although my heart sings out in imperfect tune, as when roses are in full perfect bloom. For my slender hand caresses the ivory keys, while inside my inner soul bleeds.

Dressed in red, jewelry picked to fancy any eye that has been caught in my perfect sight. Will I whisper my dreams, my goals, my deepest and darkest secrets that God will see, and all the insecurities inside of me? Night has come, as the day is no more, the love that I've dreamt was knocking at heaven's door.

My God sees me with all my flaws, and knows the day I desire to come home. For this life has become too hard, too painful, too endure. The more I cry, the more afraid, insecure woman inside of me dies.

Longing to be understood, but oftentimes very misunderstood. With her eyes closed, she thinks of walking the streets of gold. She knows she's far more worth any material things that are placed on this earth that can be sold.

Does she know who she is? Does she realize she is worth more to God than anything she could ever dream, because He's the one with the master plan. He is God. Meticulously, He created her with every single trait, her personality, and love too. She's the daughter of a King that is waiting to be freed.

Knowing that her body, mind, and soul will be treasured like pure gold. Why would she continue to sing songs in the imperfect tune, when she desires the love that will bring her to her knees. As she prays for him, they are tied by the soul.

Her heart no longer beats to that off key tune, for she listens to his heart, praying that it never parts. Joy rings down in her soul. She lays still and dreams of them as they grow old.

She loves him, although at this time she sings again out of tune, but to God it is a wonderful sound in His ear. As her tears hit the musical instrument, it too plays a sweet melody. For every tear she cries again, it has been lifted up, taking flight like an eagle gliding in the mighty wind. For the Father in Heaven, the King that still reigns on the throne collects them all when they fall.

Can a woman's heart be in perfect tune? Sure it can, if she allows the Most High to perform open-heart surgery to correct the past wounds, the broken promises, shattered dreams, and the lonely nights spent in darkness, crying as the little girl within. The little girl wants to be free, so that woman can come to the forefront and be all she can be. But before she can know her worth, she has to allow her heart to be *In Perfect Tune*.

Every Knee Shall Bow

When we sit and think about all the things that we've gone through in life; it can be more than enough for us to bow and pray. It can shield us from all hurt, harm, and danger. Take a look at the world around you. Interesting, huh? This world has been going downhill faster than we can blink our eyes. I have no other way to say it, as I think about all the things that God has taught me from my experiences.

See, so many people think that the enemy causes the pain we experience. Some of it he does. However, some of it is from the decisions we make, like not trusting God and His word for our lives. We spend too much time depending on man to give us instructions, instead of waiting on God.

Now here's an example. If we decide not to pay our car note and go out shopping instead, why get upset when the tow truck comes to pull the car. That was caused by a decision that we made. Back to the subject matter, Every Knee Shall Bow. Where I come from and how I came to be here, I know it has been nothing, but the grace of God that has helped me. As a praying woman, I know that there are still some situations that will cause you to bow at your knees in the late night hours when everyone is asleep and you have an ear to listen. There is an ear (God) that never stops listening. That alone should make your knees bow, right? But not everyone will do so.

The Bible tells us in Romans 14:11, *For it is written, As I live, saith the Lord, every knee shall bow to me, and every tongue shall confess to God.* God and his Word is more than enough!

Here is another situation. People will call and cry out to God when they are sick or when family members are ill. Why not just talk to God all the time. There are people that have not spoken to God in a long time. God is asking his people to turn back unto him quickly as the time draws near. We can see the signs of the times coming more than ever. When I was a child, I used to believe it was some fairytale about the coming of the Lord. Not until I was older, did I begin to understand.

The day I asked God to come into my heart, was when it was like heaven to me because I knew that my home was with Him and Jesus! It wasn't until I was older that I really got to know God, and every time I get a chance I bow my knees and pray, because there is **NO ONE** greater than HIM!

He is the God that is everywhere, anytime of the day, *ALL THE TIME*! At times we tend to get a little weary in our doing, because we can't see what He is doing on our behalf. But, if you just fall to your knees and begin to thank Him for all that He is, and what He will do, and worship Him; you'll begin to see some things around you change. I said that to say this: keep the faith and don't give up now because God is still on the *THRONE*. Put your faith and trust in Him. Worship Him because *HE IS WORTHY TO BE PRAISED!*

The Story of My Tears

The story of my tears rolls down my face
To express all my fears.
The broken promises, dreams, and the shattered lives
Into this liquid of surprise.
No more drama, no more pain for me hides
In the essence of quilt and shame
With each breath I take
My soul begins to shake.
I search high and I search low wondering
Where did all the time go?
Reality is my sweet destiny
The bond I share is between God and me.
For every tear that falls
He knows them all,
And begins to wipe my eyes,
Whenever I call.
Trusting in Him to guide me through,
My valleys, and make a place for me to rest in you.
It sure feels good to know that I finally aced that test
The ups and downs, on this emotional rollercoaster
have proven to be a scary ride
With many twists and turns,
Finding that there is a lesson to be learned.
For every tear that falls,
A piece of my brick wall
Is tumbling down, kneeling in prayer
It's wonderful to know that God knows
The number of my hairs.
It's amazing that God knows what
I will think before I think it.
Someday, this thing we call life will pass away,
The hugs that are no longer there

Is a bitter road of despair.
Wondering if anyone really cares,
What lead me to this place?
Could be the past,
Present or the future,
Or could be me
Wanting to be free.
Love is a funny thing,
The typical saying,
but is it the answer that lies between.
Here or there,
Taking a look around
It's everywhere.
With every single beat of my heart,
Tears flow from my eyes,
Again an element of disguise.
To be kissed with a lie brings
On the dreadful fame
Center stage for the world to see,
This person raging inside of me.
Moving on every cue,
Lord knows why I
Feel so blue.
Curtains go up, the spotlight is so bright,
That my tears are taking flight.
Unable to speak, for trying to stop every tear,
Riddled with fear.
I can feel the pain piercing
Me like a sharp spear.
Although the roads may become weary at times,
It is great to know that He is always by my side.
This too shall pass,
one day I will receive my ticket to heaven 1st class.
My tears write of a story that is so very true,
But first I must say I love you,
Do I believe what I just said,

A Portrait of Words Divinely Speaking

When all I see is frustration instead.
The image that is looking back at me,
I have forgotten who she is and why she's in so much pain
I whisper to her please let go of it,
Allow God to shield you from the cold rain.
No sight of a smile on my face,
As I turn to walk away
An angel appears to me and says
My child let us pray.
You're never alone,
Remember our father is on the Throne
There's no need to go beyond the veil,
because it has been torn.

A Heart for the Homeless

After working many years in the community assisting the homeless with food, clothing, medical assistance, toiletries and much more, I've had the opportunity to speak with homeless men, women and children from all walks of life, educated and uneducated. One of the first things that I was able to ask was this, "What are your efforts to change the current situation that you're in; in other words, "What are you doing to change your situation?" Surprisingly, the answer I received from a majority of them was the same. "If I could just find a job, a place to live and transportation then things would be so much better." Now my question was to myself was this. "How can a homeless individual obtain a job without an address, find a place to live without a job, or have reliable transportation without a job to maintain the vehicle in working condition?" Good question, huh? Honestly, that would be very difficult to do.

However, for many homeless people just the mere thought of looking for a job and depending on family to help them out with a place to stay or even transportation, can be a huge mistake on many levels. Don't get me wrong, many of them have been very grateful for the help that they have received from family; but many have been taken advantage of along the way, too. From things like paying half the rent for a spot on the couch, paying a phone bill on a phone that they never use, and here's an even better one, buying groceries for two families because they receive public assistance. Now, wait just a moment, this is the major shocker of them all: being treated less than a person just because they need help. Where is the logic in that type of help? Where is the love of God?

Here is another concern that was brought to my attention after talking with a few individuals. When they would go apply for assistance like food stamps, or medical insurance, they have been told they could get the needed help if they split up from their family. Say for instance a married couple with children. The government is eager to help more if the father is not in the home. Our society really needs to change in a major way. Or what about if the person goes to family or friends for help, then the family/friends turns them in to social services and the homeless person stands a chance of having their children taken away from them. Sometimes, no one wants to help, but yet, they claim to have all the answers. Heartbreaking right, well it is. There's not one person that is sitting pretty on a pot of gold. With the economic times continuing to fall drastically low, most of us are only one paycheck from being homeless, honestly speaking.

Without the proper agencies and caring people in place that are willing to help with these sorts of things, where does that really leave them? Let's take a look at it from a biblical side.

The Bible tells us how we should treat one another, but instead we do the total opposite. Now, Jesus being a King and coming from royalty spent a great deal of his time with the homeless and less fortunate. Take for instance the Apostle Paul who followed alongside Jesus very closely, witnessed, and endured many things. In 1 Corinthians 4:11 Paul writes: *To this very hour we go hungry and thirsty, we are in rags, we are brutally treated, we are homeless.* Now Jesus never looked down on them nor did he make them feel ashamed of their situations or circumstances; He loved and helped them.

I feel the need to share some of my story about what my family and I endured during times of hardship, which was a reason I became so passionate about doing the work of God and being an advocate for those less fortunate individuals.

Having had a family that could've done more, or even really helped us, but they did nothing! I was talked about, put down, and I became ashamed of my life and how it turned out, only because I didn't have the things that my family and I needed. Never in my wildest dreams did I ever think that my family and I would one day become homeless. Having the job skills and education, college graduates to be precise, we never went lacking. But when jobs phase out and companies cut back, what does one do? How can someone become over qualified to sweep and mop a floor or work at a fast food restaurant? It happens every day.

We have always opened our homes to family and friends when they were in need, but when we fell on hard times we endured hurtful gossip, putdowns, and were made fun of because of our situation. But you know what, to see God move in our lives in a mighty way in the midst of everything, was mind blowing. If that experience had not happened, I probably would not be writing this book, nor would you be reading it.

After spending countless nights, wondering *How is this? When will? Why did? What happened,* and all the typical questions that everyone wanted to know about the situation that we were in, I could hardly take it anymore.

Struggling for a couple of years, we still managed to produce several citywide events that catered to the needs of the homeless and less fortunate. We were able to truly meet the needs of others. This was a rewarding feeling to see lives changed by the acts of kindness. We entertain angels unaware. How wonderful is that?

We did come across an agency that was supposed to help a person or family get back on their feet, proved to be everything but that. While in that program, it became very stressful, depressing, and downright unbearable for me and my family to live in a place like that. It was a controlling environment, but we had a place to live! We were grateful, by all means. Agencies

46

like this one may proclaim to do a lot of good in the community, but to tell the truth many times they do the total opposite. I believe programs are supposed to be designed to meet the needs of each person that walks through the door. While with that particular agency, they tried to make a person become a slave because of their situation by having preposterous rules, telling them to disobey the family unit, not follow doctors' orders, or even call the clients' doctors to get them to say what they felt would be in the guidelines of their agency.

I saw so many things that were going on that nobody wanted to speak about. Even a few of the employees would try to undermine things that were totally against policies, which changed every day to suit them, but did nothing for the individuals that they claimed they were supposed to help.

The question that was asked at the beginning of this, I actually had to ask myself that same question, although my situation has changed for the better, only because God brought us out of it. I'm eternally grateful. We all should treat the homeless and less fortunate as we would like to be treated, and share the love of God. The Bible clearly tells us in Proverbs 19:17, *He who is kind to the poor lends to the LORD, and he will reward him for what he has done.*

Not trying to go so far off base here, but the efforts to make a change can be much harder than anyone could ever imagine. Now clear your mind of everything and come take a journey with me. Picture yourself being homeless, no job, and a piece of a car that is in need of major work. Then the family that's supposed to have your back, instead cause you and your family a significant amount of misery. It makes your walk even harder. That same question that was asked to another individual, I then turned around and asked myself the same question. So now, with the shoe on the other foot, here's the question again. "What efforts are you making to change the current situation that you're in?"

Well, just as I thought. No one wants to look at himself or herself as being homeless, but honestly we can't overlook it either. It is our job to care for these individuals, just as Jesus did. Think of it this way; If God created Jesus, his only son, a poor and homeless person, is it safe to say that God in actuality favors the poor and raises them.

Looking back at that agency today, the people that they serve, don't have a clue how to fight for their rights as human beings, after being stripped of everything emotionally and financially. Once they leave the program, some are in worse shape than they were when they first entered.

Let's join together and start lending a helping hand to our brothers and sisters. When we give freely without hidden agendas or wicked motives, we can bless others, including ourselves. Just remember God is always watching. We should do all we can and know to do to put a stop to this growing homeless epidemic at last.

iBelieve In Dreams

Here is a question that I am sure has crossed the minds of many people. What's the difference between *vision* and *eyesight*? The dictionary defines the word vision as a noun. *The faculty or state of being able to see, or the ability to think about, or plan the future with imagination or wisdom; a mental image of what the future will or could be like.* Now that is what the dictionary says. The dictionary defines the word *eyesight* as a noun, *a person's ability to see*. In reality, they both basically mean about the same thing. However, it's up to the individual how they receive and interpret these words.

My dreams are something that must be obtained through blood, sweat, and tears. The dictionary states the word *dream* is a noun. Being a dreamer, not always am I asleep. I have visions of things such as ideas of how I would love for things to be or the way I believe they should occur.

My dream of becoming a great writer, poet, designer, movie/play director, are not far from my reach. I have to believe and push forward to make all my dreams become a reality. Dreams can sometimes be scary, not knowing what the future holds, or if we try, will we fail. These are just a few things that float around in our minds at any time of the day. If we dare to dream, we lose out on the many possibilities of where we could go. As a firm believer of God, knowing that if we share our desires and dreams with him, He will allow us to achieve them if it is in his will. I believe God answers us in our dreams.

Thinking back over my life as teenager, I had a big dream of becoming this great singing artist. I wanted to sing and dance; tour the world. There was this show coming to town called "Putting On The Hits." I did everything I needed to do to audition. I pre-recorded myself singing on a cassette tape, so funny now since modern technology has changed drastically. Well, I received my letter in the mail, stating that they loved my tape and wanted me to come for an audition in front of the judges in my hometown. Was I excited! I was on cloud nine. Well, on the day of my audition I was unable to go. I was crushed, but I am thankful now that I didn't go that route, because had I done so, I would've missed out on some other things that I really hold dear to me, writing being one of them.

Let me bring you up to speed. I was about 14 or 15 years old. My mother and I were putting together a 1000 piece puzzle and watching a movie. I remember telling my mom that one day my name was going to go up in lights and be at the end of the movie credits with hair and makeup done by me. The things that we say as children, not knowing how powerful our tongues are. I would always say I wanted to become a hairstylist to the stars. I started doing my friends and families hair way before I was ever professionally trained. Not really looking at the bigger picture, I was not able do the hair and makeup for the movie stars, but I was able to do it for several actors and participants in plays, award shows, and fashion shows. To top that off, I was the costume technician for a few of the plays and awards shows. Being behind the scenes, I worked and planned events, not even realizing that the best was yet to come. All this time I was getting prepared on what to do, how to do it, and the right things to do. I was actually being prepared for what I am doing now.

That was a dream I had as a child, but where I'm going now is a whole different level. During those times I was writing, I never thought I would become an author, an Editor-in-Chief of my own magazine, and do freelance for other publications such as a national newspaper like the Tri-State Defender. It took a long time for me to realize that I was destined to do everything that I have done thus far.

To every soul reading these very words, whatever your dreams and desires are hold on to them for dear life. You never know when the opportunity will come and you'll be able live out your dreams. Sometimes we can have dreams of becoming the next big thing, but in God's eyes it can be a different picture playing on the big screen. Always listen to the ones that have traveled the road you are traveling, because they may have some advice that can help you. Not all advice is good so use what you can and make due.

Honestly, at the end of this life, I want to be able to say I lived out my dream(s) loud and clear. If we lose eyesight and the vision to our dream(s) it can become a nightmare, and I'm very certain we don't want that to happen. The dictionary defines *nightmare* this way: *a frightening or unpleasant dream.* Keep pushing and keep your dream(s) alive.

The Bible clearly talks about dreams and visions; so we're not too far off of that. It also tells us to write the *vision* in Habakkuk 2:2. I want to encourage you to read that in your spare time. It will bless you.

Always dream big and reach beyond what others' have deemed for you and your life. A dream is part of what we are and what we are to become. I'm yet striving to live out my dream(s) in color, bright loud color at that.

There will be people who will try to kill your dream or crush your vision, but stand on your beliefs and become "Unbreakable" as Alicia Keys sings in her song. *"We have to live our dreams like the people on TV...we have to stay tuned there's more to see... through the technical difficulties."* Wow, what a mouthful!

Believe it or not, I just started writing this and this is what happened to transpire onto paper. There was a man by the name of Dr. Martin Luther King Jr. who had given a speech titled *"I*

HAVE A DREAM." He spoke a very powerful message that he delivered on August 28, 1963 at the Lincoln Memorial in Washington, D.C. Although he didn't see what he spoke about come to pass, it's still happening to this very day. As usual, I may be getting way off base, like always, but I have to say this. Never in my wildest dream(s) would I have imagined that I would live to see an African American man lead this nation, nor did I ever dream that the first family would be. in my words, African American, just like me! Did President Obama ever dream that he would become President of the United States of America? Did his wife, First Lady Michelle, ever dream she would be the first African American woman to live in the White House or be married to the President? **DREAM BIG**! We can do it. If they did it, so can we!

For Better or For Worse?

People often overlook this when they take their vow of marriage. They are actually agreeing that no matter what will come or happen they will remain together for better or for worse, until death do them apart.

Today, nobody wants to go through the storms of life. Sometimes people think everything is always going to be a bed of roses. Honestly, when the newness of the wedding bliss wears off, reality starts to sets in. The picture becomes clear. All the moods, feelings, money, education, jobs, and family start to creep into the marriage. I've been with my spouse close to 20 years. I can say that as the family comes, health and education does too.

The vision of life, the ambitions of what I thought were going to happen, the so-called fairytale wedding, marrying so young we had no **CLUE!** We grew up very fast. It wasn't about me anymore. The things that can lead to divorce are made up of many different circumstances.

Here is a small list (I'm sure it can go on and on.)

1. Not having trust and honesty in the marriage
2. No communication
3. Lack of finances, lack of jobs or work
4. No spiritual life with God
5. Lack of education
6. Infidelity
7. Different aspects of child raising
8. Where to live or not to live
9. Health
10. Parents, caring for your parents

11. In-laws
12. Friendships
13. Abuse on all levels

If we would look at the Bible and what it tells us about marriage, many would not enter into it as fast. Marriage takes a great deal of work, time, and commitment on both parts. There is even a scripture in the Bible in *2 Corinthians 6:14* that talks about being unequally yoked. The Bible tells us what we should and shouldn't do. So many times we want what we want regardless of the cost. We have this need to want to please the flesh.

Marriage can be a very beautiful thing if both individuals work to make it that. It's just like a flower, if it is given the proper love, sunshine, and water, it will **GROW**. A lack of these things and it will wither, dry up, and die. Love takes time to develop.

There is something I found out about why the wedding ring is placed on the left hand and on the finger that it's on. Ready to be enlightened? The left hand ring finger is connected to the heart. This is an ancient tale passed down through history. I shared this because I believe it in my heart, but some people say that it is false. You heard correctly, the heart. The rings are a symbolic union between man, wife, and God! We are not supposed to be alone. God has given us instructions on our lives in that great book, the Holy Bible. This is what the word Bible means to me, *B= Basic I= Instructions B= Before L=Leaving E= Earth.*

We should be wise in all of our doing. Marriage isn't to be taken lightly. Without the correct guidance, we will run into trouble. Seek God in all things, not just marriage, but in everything that you do.

My Sister, Please Remove Your Mask

Women play a very important role in Christianity. One can say women are the backbones of churches and families. Again, in some of my previous writings, it was mentioned about the *virtuous woman*. No matter what is going on in the life of a believer of Christ, the woman always prays for her family. Through her tears, she cries out to God to strengthen her as she carries the burdens of her husband and children (if she is married with children).

As her husband being the sole provider, she baths him in prayer as he faces the world. A woman that prays does so unselfishly. She pushes and turns her plate down. She stands in the gap for her family. Oftentimes, this minority is misunderstood, mistreated, and worst of all called everything under the sun. Looking at what she endures, she's a mother before anything else, regardless of her walk with God. She's quick to act when her family needs her. God created women the way HE did for a reason. See, I believe that because women are wounded easier this is why she carries so much.

In my mid-teen years, after my mom gave her life to the Lord for the first time, I could hear her praying in the midnight hours, walking and pacing the floor for her child and her husband. Honestly, at 12am and 3am she had to be out of her mind. Was I sadly mistaken! I thank God for having such a mother that prays! It taught me how to pray and go to God with all my problems. I urge all that read this to re-examine where you are spiritually.

God is jealous, and God desires to have a relationship with each of us, but He will not force **HIMSELF** on us. A woman that prays not only prays for herself, but she prays for others. Prayer is always free. This is not to bash anyone's belief, but as for me

and my house, we will serve the Lord. ***Joshua 24:15.***
Witnessing a woman that prays in motion was indeed a sight to
see. Looking back on it now, when my mom prayed, things
changed, the atmosphere shifted. As a mother, we train up our
children in the ways they are to go. **Proverbs 22:6** clearly
instructs us on how it is to be done. When children grow-up and
leave the comfort of security, one would like to call it grace and
safety. In a world of heartache, bitterness, shame, and much
more, they find themselves going back to the one thing that was
instilled in them, and that is prayer. The power of prayer can
move mountains.

I really appreciate God for teaching me how to pray. A woman
that prays can pray life back into a person. Picture this. A woman
kneeling down on her knees with several small children pulling
and tugging on her, and her husband is standing in a place of
protection while holding the entire world on his back. Talk about
being in the right position spiritually for one another! This
woman is focused on God and not her situation. Right now, at
this point, she's looking for God to answer her prayer. Her
husband knows that she has his back, and she knows that he'll
protect her with his life. That is indeed how God intended for it
to be.

A Praying Woman is the Enemy's Worst Nightmare

Traits of A Proverbs 31 Woman

Here we go again... I have to shed a little light on our urban society. As an educated black woman, often put down, made to feel ashamed for being such, I have run across other women of color who don't feel comfortable in their skin, either because of some man, their family, or society. Television (**media**) has been the dividing force for how a woman should be typecast— as a mad black woman, ghetto, gold digging, superficial... need I say more? That's what I thought... not a pretty picture. We need to teach our daughter(s), nieces, cousins, and aunts that they are more than what this society believe them to be. Please don't get me wrong, I love the media, to a degree. After all is said and done, at the end of the day, it's what God says that we are. Look at what Proverbs 31 says:

+ *She is a woman of Virtue. Proverbs 31:10*
+ *She is a woman of Faithfulness. Proverbs 31:11*
+ *She is a woman of Reverence. Proverbs 31:12*
+ *She is a woman of Goodness. Proverbs 31:12*
+ *She is a Willing Worker. Proverbs 31:13*
+ *She is a Good Manager. Proverbs 31:14,15*
+ *She is Industrious. Proverbs 31:16*
+ *She is a woman of Strength. Proverbs 31:17*
+ *She is a woman of Endurance. Proverbs 31:18*
+ *She is Well Rounded. Proverbs 31:19*
+ *She is Charitable. Proverbs 31:20*
+ *She is a Provider. Proverbs 31:21*
+ *She is well dressed. Proverbs 31:22*
+ *She is the Wife of a Good Husband. Proverbs 31:23*
+ *She is a Good Business woman. Proverbs 31:24*
+ *She is Honorable. Proverbs 31:25*
+ *She is Wise. Proverbs 31:26a*
+ *She is Kind. Proverbs 31:26b*

+ *She is a Good Mother. Proverbs 31:27a*
+ *She is a Woman After God's Own Heart!*

Now why would we want to be anything less than what God has created us to be?

We need to teach and lead other women by example. We need to understand that **THE HEAVENLY FATHER THAT REIGNS IN HEAVEN** said we are his precious jewels. We must know our value and our worth. Wait just one minute because it gets better. When God created Adam, it was good. He saw his loneliness and that was not good. He created Eve, which means they were created in God's image and his physical likeness, so why would mainstream society tell us otherwise? Well, for one everything that God created is and was good, so the enemy's job is to do the total opposite of that.

There are so many women who change parts about their physical body, like their breasts, lips, cheekbones, and buns of steel implants…for what? If we stop playing into this foolishness and accept how HE created us, then we can take our rightful place in God!

Some may find this being a little too bias. So what? I have a right to say what I want to say and do what I want to do. No, I am not judging anyone or anybody. I'm just telling the truth, I want all that God has for me, and I want to be all that **HIS WORD** says I can be. The **WORD OF GOD** does not lie nor will it come back to him void.

People get it so twisted from fact to reasoning. Basically justifying why they do wrong, like one sin is greater than the other. Really? Genesis 39:9 clearly says that *There is none greater in this house than I; neither hath he kept back anything from me but thee, because thou art his wife: how then can I do this great wickedness, and sin against God?* Let's look at

Matthew 5:19 which says, *Whosoever therefore shall break one of these least commandments, and shall teach men so, he shall be called the least in the kingdom of heaven: but whosoever shall do and teach them, the same shall be called great in the kingdom of heaven.*

I have been saying different things on my Facebook posts that have gotten some very *not so nice* comments, which I deleted. I'm not trying to pretend to be this great spiritual expert, whatever that is, but I do obey what the spirit of the Lord directs me to tell HIS people. First of all, when the message is deposited and downloaded to me, I have to deal with it first, then after I'm done patting myself up from crying and asking God why me, I follow his direction. My Facebook page is my page. It is where I express what is on my mind. No, I did not go there to make enemies. It's one thing when you know the truth and it's staring you right in the face. Thank God for Jesus. Honestly speaking, I am only a vessel that God chose. If I could have my choice of jobs, I would have allowed it to pass me by. Thank God again for the chasing. God takes us through many things for our making. We have to understand **HE KNOWS WHAT IS BEST FOR YOU AND ME.**

There was this one status that I posted where I was talking about opening up our homes and lives to the attacks of the enemy, such as, allowing our children, with very impressionable minds, to over indulge into this wickedness of television like adult censored cartoons. I may be getting off here, but this needs to be said. I have watched Family Guy and American Dad; I will only name these two. After doing some research and studying the creator of these shows, I discovered that he supports various community issues on same-sex relationships. I didn't know this at first. Talk about an eye opener. I know what the **BIBLE** says about that. How can I support someone who supports the opposite of what God has designed? We all need to be very mindful of the things we entertain; because at the end of the day we will be held accountable for what we do or do not do.

When we know what's right we tend not to acknowledge it, for accountability is placed with us. **REAL TALK -** I'm coming straight from the hip. Let's take our communities back and fight for what should be.

And above all things have fervent charity among yourselves: for charity shall cover the multitude of sins. 1 Peter 4:9. Please know that I'm not passing judgment on anyone. I am just saying that a picture is worth a thousand words, or better yet, actions speak louder than words. We can't begin to express ourselves, but we do just that in what we wear. Take this for an example, growing up, I used to hear this saying, too, *"You will never really know until you've walked a mile in my shoes"* Many of us can wear the same shoe size, but can we walk in the other person's shoes? Personally, maybe and maybe not. Why try to walk in shoes that are too big, too wide, or too narrow? I'm sure you get it.

I believe we try to fit into places that we never were meant to fit into. Think about it. Remember being told by your parents not to wear someone else's shoes? There was a reason for that. I think hygiene had a lot to do with it then. My shoes are hard enough trying to walk in let alone, me trying to walk in someone else's.

We may admire the shiny four or five-inch platforms with ankle straps, adorned with rhinestones, size seven and half. Actually that would be too small for me, and besides, I don't want to break my neck trying to pretend that I have it all together. I believe one day, even the person walking in them will realize they're not safe. No I'm not saying that to be mean, I give props to those that can. I'm just saying at the end of the day, when they're all alone, guess what? The shoes do come off and they even question why they bought them in the first place.

Each and every shoe that we own, just like us, they have their own story. You look at shoes and remember what you did in them or what you had to get away from. Look down at your shoes. Some have seen better times, but you hold on to them, but why? Maybe to remind you of where you came from, or maybe where you're going and maybe even desire to go. Only you can tell. We have shoes for every occasion. Some for jeans, some for going to the park or out for a night on the town. We buy them to make us feel better when we've had a bad day or because we want to treat ourselves to something nice once in a while, or to make that outfit **POP**!

Regardless of the reason why you buy them, why do people see your shoes before they see you? That is a question I would like to know myself. Now if we would like to walk a mile in someone else's shoes we really need to look at ourselves in the mirror, search in our eyes and answer the question why?

As I said before, I have too many things going on in my life to try to put my foot in someone else's shoes. I recall this other saying, *"Walk in my footsteps."* Are you kidding me! I know that at some point in time this has got to come to an end sooner or later. We can spend all day trying on shoes, and may even stop by a friend's house and go through their closet, looking for a pair of shoes. But guess what, although they may fit, something about that shoe will never be right. One, it may be worn down on the heel, which will give you a slight lean or you can feel where their toes have made its imprint into the shoe. When looking for the right shoe, take your time. Don't buy the first shoe you lay your eyes on. You'll know when you see it, literary speaking, though.

Does it matter how much you spend on your shoes? To me, I would say *no*! Just make sure they are the right color, size, and style for the season. Before you know it you could end up with the most ugly pair of shoes that don't go with anything.

The Younger Generation

What does it takes to become a great leader? It takes a great deal of honesty, respect, tact, dedication, and the fortitude to want to be a great leader. There are many characteristics that should display a great leader, such as being a good listener, willing to allow individuals the opportunity to grow under your leadership. A great leader recognizes strengths and weaknesses in the people that they are leading. They will make sure that those they lead reach their potential.

A leader has to be able to follow before he or she can lead anyone else. Understand what it means to be a leader, and not a drill sergeant. A great leader will have favor with the people that they lead. A person in leadership will not display negative behavior; they will be kind and willing to help. Leaders will not act as though they own those that are under their authority, whether it's a job, community, government or religion based.

I can remember being in school. We had to take turns to be the line leader; I know I'm going down memory lane. Imagine how powerful you were when it was your turn to lead. What a wonderful feeling, huh? Yes! You make sure that the line is straight. You hold the door for everyone. With that job, you had to be on your best behavior at all times, because if you didn't you would lose your turn. There's really no difference here. Leaders are made.

Remember the game follow the leader and everyone wanted to be the leader. Well, not everyone is made to be a leader. There is an old saying, *"Leaders are made, not born."* In my opinion, I see it both ways. Some people are natural leaders and others can be groomed to become great leaders.

A great leader will own up to their shortcomings, apologize when a mistake has been made, and is willing to go the extra mile for those that he or she has charge over. If we look at the Bible, there were some great leaders, and even in our history books.

We have the perfect leader of all times. His name is Jesus. This is a man perfect in every way. He led a multitude of individuals. He even allowed them the opportunity to grow; He led by example. Jesus had all the characteristics of a great leader. He came to serve and gave up His life for us. A King! Never did he question what His role was when He came to the world. Then there was David, a man after God's own heart. To have the seal of approval from God, that is a high recommendation, in my opinion.

Leaders should stand by their words and not waiver under subjection. To become a great leader one shouldn't throw his or her title around to make someone else feel unimportant. There's a saying, *"I respect your title, but I don't have any respect for you as a person."*

President Obama, being the leader of this country, has to follow the laws of the land and govern himself accordingly. Even though he runs the country, he still has to get approval on things that he wants changed. Oftentimes we are so hung up on titles and positions that we forget about what's on the agenda.

Let's take a look at the individuals that own and run their own companies. Most of the time they change policies to benefit themselves and their company, and not the people that they employ. What happens when they develop a bad reputation in the community and others don't want to be under their leadership? Those leaders have proven to be out for selfish game. To be a great leader one needs to follow through with their mission statement. We need to teach our future leaders of tomorrow how it should be done.

Here's another situation. What if you had the opportunity to be head of a major project? Your job is to oversee the operation from start to finish. You're looking for a team of people to assist you in doing so. After much planning, you receive an email stating that you have a few people that would like to take part in it, but memos were already sent out to those that were interested in becoming part of the team. After the ones that adhered to the memo followed through with responding to deadlines, what do you do? Do you allow others the opportunity to join after deadlines have been given and change the rules to accommodate those that want to jump on board after the fact? That is unfair to you as the leader of the project and the individuals that responded in a timely manner. However you could very well lose credibility within the company, and others might label you as a bad leader. Others might say that they no longer want to do business with you or you can't lead them anywhere. How would you handle it? The way I would choose to settle the situation would be as such. My reply would say something like this: *I have already selected those that will assist me. However, in the near future there may be other opportunities for you to participate. I thank you for wanting to be part of this project.* Now that's how that should be handled. People will respect you for handling it properly. This is what displays a great leader. So, if you're a leader and aren't acting as such, then maybe it's time to change and do the right thing.

Where Are You?

A lot of things run wildly throughout my mind, feelings of confusion, tiredness, and mental abandonment. To know that I've called out to you with little to no response, my heart is longing to feel your love near me. My mind is full of trouble, as this world we live in becomes more and more chaotic.

There is talk of the New World Order, everything becoming one. Standing on the wall looking as the world crumbles and falls. So much is happening and people don't seem to mind at least one bit. These tears that I try to hold back are in a race to see who will hit the floor first.

There are a lot of people wondering the same thing. I'm asking, where are you? The love that you have for us as your children runs deeper than we can ever imagine, but we return much less than what you give. Yet, you still bless us one by one. It's just those times when things don't make since, I'm still looking around asking, *where are you?*

My logic knows what's been said to me many times before, that you're always with me. I feel so far away from your presence when I'm in distress. Can barely catch my breath.

I don't understand why, seeming how much time is flying bye. The prayers I send you somehow seem to be hitting the ceiling, and hitting me on the top of my head. I pray for strength, joy, peace, and rest. Never looking for material things, I just want to be closer to you than ever before, as close as Heaven's door.

This heart is bleeding and crying for the nations, the children our leaders of tomorrow. We need you right now. Father, can you hear me? I'm listening for your voice and your people need you too. *Where are you?*

Swollen eyes, stopped up nose, head is pounding like a drummer beating his drums. What do I need to do to hear a word from you? Reading my Bible to know more of you, I want to feel your touch. All we need is just one touch. If you would just touch me, I know that my life will be changed forever.

Father, please hear my plea, as I seek your face for direction in what I must do next. I have tried everything. Sometimes nothing seems to work for me. What I thought I knew that's not it anymore. I seem to be losing it. Father, *where are you?*

I need answers about what is going on around me and in this world. *Where are you?* I know you hear me, but why am I not hearing you? *Where are you?* I love you, I adore you, and you are the head of my life. What else can I do to be closer to you? *Where are you?*

Beauty 101

Let's talk about it. As you may know there are many articles, stories, and commercials about hair and skin care. People are always saying try this or do that. However, being a professional I opted out of feeding others foolishness.

First things first…

Taking care of your body from the inside will show on the outside. I have been in the same circle, trying new products, trying to achieve something that was already there. When it comes to hair and skin, natural is always better. I really believe that once we start to fix things that aren't broken we mess up. I would always try to convince people to get away from doing unhealthy things to their hair and skin. Simple things and all natural things are always best.

Our bodies aren't designed to take all of the harsh chemicals we put in it or on it. Don't get me wrong, there's nothing wrong with a bit to enhance your appearance. I believe that when you find the peace in who you are and who God created you to be that's all that matters.

When I was a cosmetology instructor, there were things everyone was so in a rush to try, such as applying chemicals to their skin and hair. Although the book would say its fine, I would explain to them that they were in the business to take care of the hair, not destroy it. Shampoo and condition on a regular basis, and eat properly to maintain your overall health. I educated my clients on this, too. It paid off in the long run. They were happy with the results, and so was I along with the fact that my business grew. I've even been told that it's more money doing chemicals; which that is so very true, but I would rather not do that.

I'm into everything natural. I've managed to make all of my beauty products from lip balms, black soap shampoo, black soap facial wash, whipped Shea butter mix for my hair and leave-in-conditioners all from natural ingredients. One day I plan to live life fully and embrace the things that God has blessed me to have.

We really should consider what we place into our bodies, too. Remember the old saying, "You are what you eat?" That is so true on every single level. Just drinking water promotes healthy skin and hair.

Take the time out to eat a well-balanced meal, get enough exercise and rest, and the body will be just like a well-oiled machine. That is the total package, mind, body, and soul. Take time out to care for yourself naturally now and your body will take care of you in the end. Be sure to love yourself first inside and out.

Prophetic Chatter

God truly is up to something. There has been a shifting taking place right now. Just because you're going through something doesn't mean that you've messed up somewhere along the path. How many times have I heard, "You need to get it together?" My God! Education, jobs/careers, friends, family, etc., does not keep you from going through something in life.

Life happens, some good and some bad, but God gets the glory. I'm not defined by any of that. I am defined by what God has written about my life. I am no longer suffering from of an identity crisis. Don't place a label on anyone. God is the reason, why I live another level in Christ.

Today has been such a good day. I managed to get a lot of things done. The hours have flown by so fast, but who is complaining when you are having fun in the process. I love it. If you only knew what I do in the course of my days. God, let your perfect will be done in me, through me, and keep me on the potter's wheel! Not my will, but yours.

I have been dreaming about weddings for the past several weeks. Get ready people of God. He's coming for his bride. Dress rehearsal, gown fittings, and the table has been prepared. *WILL YOU BE READY TO DINE WITH THE FATHER? A ROYAL WEDDING IS ABOUT TO TAKE PLACE.*

"Wake up now! The invitations have been sent," said the Lord. Special invitations. Sleeping Beauty arise. Will you say *I Do*?

Spiritual Conversation

Changing the course of history starts with first, writing it. Leave a legacy behind for your children and family to enjoy for years to come, just like a photo album. When company comes over, you pull out that big box and laugh at the goofy clothes. Just laughing at what was going on during that time when the moment was captured within that lens.

Keep the memories alive. I'm sitting here, looking out of the window, listening to the splatter of rain on the window sill, thinking of the many times, when I would sit for hours on end just writing until my heart's deepest treasures began to cover the pages of my journal.

Time would have passed by, as I would be so in tune with my thoughts and my favorite pen/journal curled up in the bed or sitting on the couch. I would spill my heart and guts for hours, I even find it funny at times too, my visions and dreams as a child, and actually witnessing them happen. If there is ever anything that is of value, put it in a book, in your own very words.

Divinely Speaking through my pen, iSpeak, iCreate & iPen™ *My_Journey_In_A_Book*. OKAY. You have to love this! I am so laughing. Where do thoughts like these come from? I'm guessing, inside my mind. The analytical systems deemed with streams of thoughts to capture the vast of social media as it spreads like wild fire through the digital DNA of transmitted signals to communicate to one network to another. Internet, mobile devices, emails, video streaming, and so much more. Does anyone understand this? Because I am so laughing over here!

You Are My Adam and I Am Your Eve

Divinely Speaking. This was a random poem that I decided to pen, as I was lost in the midst of my thoughts. It sure is wonderful you can share what God gives you while you're in a place to hear Him speak.

My open letter to you, Adam.

You are my Adam and I am your Eve. Adam of old, though you were asleep, a place of intimacy with the Father because God wanted to speak to you concerning the very life and the wife that he gave you, (me). Built to stand in agreement, to be fruitful and multiply. That we are to live off of what God supplies. Not for me to be looking for other things to be tempted by what I see, but for your love and direction and walking in total fellowship with Him to lead me to Him. Prior to my arrival into the earth realm, I was created to take my position as bone of your bone, flesh of your flesh. You called me **WOMAN** because I was taken from your rib to walk in love and to be a helpmeet to you. By your side I stood, even when you accused me of deceiving you. But you were made the Head, not me. Yes, I made a mistake. I realized that, but I, too, blamed someone else for getting off track. It's better when the joke is not on you. Together, we both brought forth life into the earth. God has blessed us, even before we became a pair. The one that became two, which was you and me, predestined you see.

You are my Adam and I am your Eve. Together we made history. We have left behind a beautiful legacy for our children, and their children to see, what true love really should be.

You are my Adam and I am your Eve. Even though we faced many trials and tribulations, God still brought us through. We've suffered the consequences of following after things that weren't in His will, but He did get the glory and has rewritten our love story. This is truly our love story. Together, we remain.

You are my Adam, no longer asleep. I am your Eve, let's wake up and walk together spiritually and believe. There was no question if I was your wife. You knew, and understood the will of our Father. You obtained favor from God. I was placed here for you, not the other way around. As I would sit at a distance and watch you work in the fields, to bring us such a tasty meal, to fill our bellies, and rest under trees, in the cool of the evening, when life was so simple and quiet easy. Then one day, things took a drastic turn for the worst. Out of our disobedience, it brought on a curse. A curse that neither you or I were able to run from. Only into the presence of our Father, who knew what we'd done. Hiding from his voice, we stood in Judgment and faced that music, you know the instrument of the blame game, who did what, and why? Evicted out of the place that was given unto us, we gave up what had been given freely to us all for just a bite of what appeared to be delightful in sight, but death to our soul. Sweet in smell and taste, can you believe how we made our Father feel? Sorry, comes from the bowels of my heart and the depths of my soul, I should have been somewhere fasting and praying. Bathing our marriage and family in prayer.

You are my Adam and I am your Eve! Your touch warmed even my soul. The reflection of you in my eyes reminds of the days of our first meeting. You called me Eve.

Sweet Aroma

This was like the smell of sweet rain
True freshness, the true fruit from his vine
Thank you for sharing with me, as you always do
The words that pour so freely from your pen
To pen or inscribe the heartbeat of our Father.
To be summoned by The King.
In the bridal chambers
He awaits for our arrival,
Our worship,
And our prayer
As we minister to him.
Adorned, he clothed us in his righteousness.
Our prayers are a sweet smelling savor unto his nostrils
As he breathes.
For Him we live and move.
Our father is moved
by our willingness to pen.
God bless you!

Arise Men

What does a real man look like? Yes, that would be a question that I'm asking. Trying to define what his appearance would be is hard for many of us to visualize. Frankly, does he have a face? What I uses to envision as a little girl was my father. He was my Superman. He could do **NO** wrong. He was the **IT** in my book. As I grew older and wiser, I learned that we all have character flaws. There is only one man that exemplifies what a man should be; his name is Jesus! He was a man that knew no sin. A man who did nothing wrong. He was an honest man that worked for a living. He gave his life for another, which happened to be us. Jesus cared for the sick and the poor. This would be a perfect role model for any man or woman to follow. Jesus was kind and compassionate to those that He encountered on a daily basis.

I honestly believe that there could be real men among us; however, I believe that a man can be trained to become a real man and even look like one as well. In my case, my husband has truly exemplified that in the lives of our children. He provided the nurturing that each of us needed. His love for us was the most important of all.

And to think, a real man should wear his pants pulled up with a belt! I believe a man should be a hard worker, a great provider, and a warrior for his family. I believe that a man will train his son how to treat his wife or girlfriend, how he should be with his family in public, and behind closed doors.

A modern day super hero will not allow society to determine who he is in God and how far he can go in life. Many African American men face the brutal reality of being deemed as deadbeats, low life, stupid, unlearned, and lazy (this checklist could go on for days). Let's visit our media, like the news. Huh, yep, the news sensationalizes all the negativity of our men in general. It doesn't matter the social status, education, or career of choice the media will find fault in any and everything when it comes to the order, which God set. What better way to destroy God's design and plan than by hurting the men that God created.

If the majority of these young men between 16- 30 years of age had places to go to be mentored, encouraged, and loved 99% of them wouldn't have committed the crimes that they have committed. With the budget cuts of the Boys' Club, Cub Scouts, community sports leagues, church organizations, and after school activities, what is there to do, other than get into trouble?

I believe that we should all pitch in to help our young men get the nurturing they need to become outstanding **MEN OF VALOR and INDIVIDUALS** that **GOD** would have them to be!

Let's take a few minutes out of the day to say a kind word to a young man other than telling him that he will never amount to anything. The Bible tells us there is life and death in the tongue and we should control it before we really do some serious damage to their spirit. We need to help them and not hurt them.

A man will go before God for direction in life in order to lead his family. Man Up! Man was created in God's image, not in the image of man.

Practice What You Preach

So many times, we tell our children to behave and for them not to do things that will get them into trouble. How can we preach these things and we're doing the very thing that we tell them not to do? For instance, how can a mother tell her daughter not to have sex before marriage, but yet the mother is having a different guy in the house and wants to get upset when the daughter is acting just as she's being taught.

The fathers are not getting off by a long shot. You tell your son to respect women, but yet and still you disrespect his mother, or any other woman that passes by talking under her clothes. As parents, we need to be careful and mindful of the messages we send to our children. We are the very reason so many of them are acting like they have no earthly sense that God has given them. Yet, they belong to the Lord, so we have to allow the Holy Spirit to do the work that needs to be done in their lives as well as our own.

On the flipside of things, God tells us parents how we are to train our children in the book of Proverbs 22:6. *Train up a child in the way he should go: and when he is old, he will not depart from it.* I can honestly say that when I got older I, for one, never forgot what my parents taught me about the Word of God. My mother taught me that if I ever got in trouble that I could call on the name of Jesus and He would be right there to answer me. The Bible even tells us in Ephesians 5:25, *Husbands, love your wives, even as Christ also loved the church, and gave himself for it.* We see clearly in this text that God left great instructions on how we should conduct ourselves in life. Ephesians 5:22 says, *Wives, submit yourselves unto your own husbands, as unto the Lord.*

God was telling us that the way we present ourselves to Him we have to do the same thing toward our husbands.

We should thank God for another opportunity to get it right. Lord knows that I'm grateful. As people of God that were created in His image, we should do everything possible to please Him. If we stop trying to please man and please God we will be on the right track.

There is something I never really understood, how can we hate one another and profess to love God? John 4:20 it states, *If a man says, I love God, and hateth his brother, he is a liar: for he that loveth not his brother whom he hath seen, how can he love God whom he hath not seen?*

This is how I came up with the title **Practice What You Preach**. We really should look in the mirror and not just talk about doing the right thing, but indeed be about God's business. As a believer, I believe that God sent Jesus, His son, who knew **NO SIN** to die for me as well as you. Here's something to think about.... Could you ever repay God for what He did for you? He gave His son, which was His very best, for us. Are you willing to give Him your best?

Willing To Be Used by God

One evening, husband and I went out to make a store run. There is this little antique shop that I have been wanting to go inside and just look around. *So, here's the story.*

I walked around the store just looking and admiring a lot of things that were really old like chairs, tables, and knickknacks. Meanwhile, hubby went to the store and was going to come back to get me. Anyway, I asked the owner a few things about lay-ways just to strike up a conversation, while his wife was on the phone. I walked a bit closer so I could hear him because the both of them were elderly. I know they were over 75 years old because he said after 75 years of age his wife said, "We can go back to work." He laughed.

In the midst of the conversation, he began to share with me all the many health problems that his wife had, including breast cancer. I kept listening, and never really put two and two together. Holy Spirit reminded me that I had seen this man three weeks prior at Wal-Mart, returning some merchandise because it was missing something out of the box. Why am I saying this? Well, here's where it gets very special.

Now as I was talking to them both, two cats walked up, and I made mention of them. He said, "They are hungry. We feed them everyday." As he got up to feed the cats, his wife started explaining to me why he had on a black with pink trim sweater cap.

Honestly, I saw it, but I didn't see it, but since she said something about the cap, I looked. She told me that he recently had surgery on his ear because of cancer, and part of his ear was removed.

"Sometimes you may have to talk loud so he can hear, and he may at times talk over you, because he can't hear you that well," his wife said.

I heard Holy Spirit say, *pray for him*! This was totally out of my comfort zone, yet once again, this is where I was reminded about seeing him weeks before, not even knowing that we would cross paths again. I noticed the bandage on the side of his head even then, and thought, *I wonder what happened?*

I asked him if he would mind if I prayed for him, and he said he could always use prayer! I then turned in the direction of where his wife was sitting, and she said yes, too! Then she said, "My son always says prayer is power!"

I agreed, "Yes, ma'am, it is."

So her husband went on to feed the cats. By this time, my husband pulls up. I asked him to come inside and we both prayed for them. I went over to the elderly man, I took his hand into my hand, and I began to pray for him. He started to squeeze my hand. I continued to pray, and once I finished, they both thanked me.

As, we were turning to walk out the door, the wife asked me if I was a preacher. I laughed, smiled, and said, "Yes, ma'am."

She said, I could tell as you were praying. I heard it all in your voice."

I was about to cry because they really blessed me. I was going for one thing, because what I went into the store to see, which was a purple desk, wasn't even in the store. I thought it was gone, but turns out it was outside covered up by other furniture. God had a different plan. God always sets us up to do work in the

Kingdom. I would have never in my life moved like this before. I thank God for the pushing. Otherwise, I would have simply prayed for them when I got home or in the car.

Sometimes Father just wants to physically touch his people through his earthen vessels. Moments later, when we passed back by the store, I mean a matter of five minutes, they were closed!

We tend to talk all the time, saying we really want God to use us, but we miss the opportunity to touch God's people because it's not in a certain place, and I'm sure we all know what that means. I thank God for leading and guiding me, and pushing me out of my comfort zone. Today I brought hope to His son and daughter.
One of the best things during my life that has helped me to cope through some really hard times, when I was so unsure about everything is to write poems, notes, and letters to people. I never went anywhere without paper and pen. Journaling has been my lifeline. I could share my thoughts on paper without being judged for it.

There was a time when I lost the will or love to write, when writings were discovered and I was punished for what I had written. I had to be in my mid-teens. I went through a lot at that time. I kept it bottled up for years. It wasn't until I was in my early 20's that I picked up a pen again. Looking at it now, I was called to write because of the struggle and what I had to go through to get to this place. I found peace and safety in my journals; I could say what I needed to say without ever having to explain my writings because they belonged to me.
Because I am very protective of what I share when it comes to my writings, it's like a baby to me and I will protect it.

I want to encourage you to keep writing. Never allow anyone to tell you otherwise. If writing helps you to get from point A to point B, write. Journal about your journey. God sees and he knows all! He wants to hear from you in the midst of your processing. It has brought me healing. May God's love prompt you to pen, to leave behind a legacy of how God saw you through the struggles.

Love Story Revealed

I believe the greatest love story ever written is about the Love that God has concerning the life that He preordained for me. Sometimes it just amazes me how he communicates his never-ending, unfailingly, and unconditional love for me each day of my life. Perfect, I am not! But a Holy God saw fit to love the most imperfect things in all my imperfections.

The attention to every detail that God has written concerning who I am in Him, his very fabric of **DNA** has made my life possible. Excuse me, but I am having a moment right now. My God, the least that I can do is love Him and follow the strategic plans for the life He's given me.

To deny my God-given qualities, characteristics, and compassion is like not being oneself. I want the story that God is penning concerning my life to have the perfect ending.

You can't keep ignoring God. Eventually he will have his way. You can either accept Him now, willingly, or have something drastic cause you to accept Him. It is up to you to trust God. Only the things for God will last. Anything besides that is temporary. I would rather have God's blessings!

Freedom

Sometimes in order to move forward into the things of God, you must let go of the toxicity, whether it's people, places, things, ideas, or mindsets that are buried deep down in the inside of you. Time to get in a place to be purged of what is trying to stay around to keep you ill and stagnated. Some things do take time, and time does heal wounds. The important thing to remember is you have to want it just as much as you want to be free. This is another process that takes time and continued deliverance.

I've often thought about how far I could have been in life if I'd done a few things differently! Then I thought what if I hadn't gone through what I did, would my relationship with God be any different now? Honestly, when I decided to listen to God, and stop listening to the opinions of other people about what they thought God was saying to them concerning me, when I know I hear from the Lord for myself, it was a smooth transition for me. My God what freedom, even when it feels a little uncomfortable.

I've tried to live a life pleasing to others, even if I was unhappy, the more I tried, the harder it became for me. I shutdown totally. I began to cut people off; I mean write them out of my life as if they didn't even exist. God knows that wasn't me at all, but you know I went through a phase that I thought giving everything I had in me, like my time, my friendship, my generosity, my kindness, and heart, all the while I was struggling to be free. It would actually make people like me, but how much more emptier I became. They only cared about themselves and what I could do for them, totally not what God wanted me to be doing. Then I realized and thought, people only wanted me around because of what I was able to do or could do for them. I'm only sharing this because I am led of the Lord to do so. It does matter about who you're connected to because everyone doesn't desire your friendship as much as you desire theirs. You literally have to release them to God, and **FORGIVE THEM!** That seven-letter word is a hard one! The best way for me to describe it, and handle it is like this.

F =	Freedom
O =	Obedient
R =	Release
G =	God
I =	Intimacy
V =	Virtue
E =	Eternity

So, I need **freedom** to be **obedient** to **release** everything to **God**, in the **intimacy** of prayer and my love time in his presence, to be able to receive healing **virtue** of His love for all **Eternity**.

A Letter of Love

Oftentimes, it could seem like a great deal
Of distance between you and I
But you understand my every single cry,
You take the time to collect my tears
And comfort me from all my fears.
God, you are my rock and dearest love
And you secured my fate
My love for you grows greater each and every day.
Your banner is love over me
And your wings cover and protect me.
Psalm 23 says
That you make me to lie down
In green pastures,
A story that explains Father knows best
When my body is tired, you cause me to rest.
Whisked away into the secret chambers to listen
To the stillness of your voice
Deep asleep, I have no choice.
The things you share with me
I am in a complete daze
As you reveal your path and your gentle ways.
Visions that dance in my eye-gates
Is a wonder to see that there's
not such a great distance between YOU and me.
Through my pen iSpeak, iCreate and iPen
The truth of my relationship with YOU
I'd have it no other way by any chance.
See what I dreamed about is
Sweet and pure romance
The joy within my soul shivering cold
You removed the black and bitter coal
From what was once my darkened soul.

Clean I am because of your love for me
That was paid on Calvary.
A debt that was settled
With the shedding of your son's blood
How remarkable, mixing spit and clay to restore
The sight of a man, you are worthy of praise.
He was excommunicated from those
That didn't understand miracles, signs, and your
Wonderful wonders
Here I am to speak of many
Things you did just for me
With my pen in my hand
Everything You did was all in your plan.
The visions that I had in the past
Which I didn't quite get, have now become
My vivid reality.
I don't always know what to make of it
But it is you I seek to please
The protector of me.
God, you have been
My drive as I search the heavens
High beyond the big blue skies.
Where the white clouds
Hang and your beauty still remains.
To have my body warmed by the sun
And my skin kissed by the wind
As I am listening to your voice from within
God, you are My Master, My Father and My Friend
You always make time for me
As I kneel in prayer to thee.
I'm thankful that you have the keys to my heart.
Loving you has been difficult at times,
But as I have learned of you
And answered your call,
Loving you isn't hard at all.
In you, I became a jewel so precious

To see that I saw myself as the true apple of your eye.
There is peace and security in you
Not the counterfeit that I've often seen.
YOU are the real deal
And everything in between.
God, please take my hand
and lead me as we dance,
The audience of one, the intimacy the Father/Daughter dance
I have been adorned in clothing to bless you my King
You spin me around as the angels sing.
You are seated on the throne and
I am in heaven, no more alone.
In my dress
I leap and I twirl before you,
Because you have seen me through.
How I've longed to be with you
And walk the streets of gold
This vision of heaven has often been told,
And never grows old.
There's nothing that keeps me from you
I'm thankful for your love
It's ever so true.
This is my dedication to you,
A Letter of Love

GRACE

Grace is the evidence of You calling me close to you; to teach me your ways for you are the ancient of days.

Grace is love that covers me from the sweet dew that gentle glistening upon the grass, knowing that trouble will not last, and this too shall pass.

Grace is the fragrance that dances to the melodic sound of the wind, orchestrated by the strings that are picked on a violin.

Grace is the sunrise in the distant east and the settling of the illuminated moonlight with the twinkling of sparking stars that float in the midnight sky.

Grace is the stillness in your voice that causes me to seek your face and deeper realms of You that are unknown, what a vision I have of you sitting on the throne.

Grace is the flowing of the rivers, brooks, creeks, and shallow streams, for as wide as the ocean deep as the sea, my love for YOU, Heavenly father goes beyond my wildest dreams.

Grace canvases the earth here and there; no other comes close to you, YAH, and cannot be compared. Because of your love, my life was spared

Grace has found my heart and sheltered it from the frigid cold, as I'm reminded of the most beautiful love story that was ever told; that was given the authority, to speak your word bold.

Grace knows of my existence in life. Your wisdom I seek and justified by your love for me. I penned this poem to see You as my Elohim that will return as reigning King, while the angels in heaven sing.

Grace is so close to me that it radiates that I am to allow You to shine for time has stood still, and I am reminded that I must remain on "The Potter's Wheel" so you can complete the work that you started in me. You are rewriting my story. You are the author and finisher of my faith

Grace is abundance, faith, and truth that I have found in You, leaning not to my own understanding that would be foolish to do. **Grace** was designed to keep me free from all of my enemies.

Grace is sufficient enough, there's no need for a substitute when in You I found the solution, you see. Not like before, when I was coming up empty, by running away from the life that you promised me.

Grace is You that multiplied your people, divided nations and seas, subtracted sin from our record and added the gift of Salvation, equaling your love manifested.

Grace is what brought me to this conclusion, that seeing the unseen through your eyes, for the knowledge of Christ. His mind is in me, I rose with him and I will reign with him for all eternity.

Pondering moment that I died before I was sent into the earth, I am here to do a greater work. To speak your word in truth without compromise, because you came to set the captives free. All I have to do is remain on the path that you preordained for me. I'm determined to walk in purpose and destiny that is my portion, quite honestly.

Separating fact from fiction, how can this be, when there's no truth in all of Satan's lies you see. Life and death is truly a reality. You must believe that there is a penalty. The wages of sins is death. None of us was there when Jesus wept.

Grace causes me to surrender my **ALL**, to trust in **YAH**, because He will see me through. I have learned to truly depend on you, not in what I see.

Grace teaches me how to abide in **YOU**, because you laid down your life for me. By what you did on Calvary.

Misunderstood

I became decomposed to the reality of truth about who God called me to be. Often fighting my calling deep inside my soul that I became opposed. Rejected, Projected, Subjected and Neglected to deal with the love that was waiting for me. See I closed off any feelings of affection anyone showed me. It was always with obligation. That lead to separation and I began to war heavily in retaliation.

Numb to affection, numb to love, numb to speak, when deep inside my soul was weak. Having those one on one talks with God, opened the intimacies of a wounded heart. Having my voice stolen, how do I regain it now? I speak to you in divine truth. Sometimes I wonder what did I do to deserve such treatment like this, Lord?

What did I miss? My voice was silenced in my youth as well, because no adult wanted to face the truth. Opened up to emotional pain, when I thought my cries to him went in vain.

Time and time again, I prayed for death, but His love overshadowed me in the end. My mind drifted a time or two, thinking about what did I have to do, to tell what I know and not be punished for what happened to me.

Christ went to the cross to seek and save the lost. I was broken and badly abused, but Jesus' love healed my wounds. One of the things I really became good at was pretending to be okay. That way I could keep people at bay.

At age nine, or maybe younger, I had my eyes opened to every bit of wickedness and sexual perversion that came to pollute and cause me to abort this assignment that had been placed within. I longed for a love that didn't know I existed. Don't get me wrong, I know it sounds twisted.

I was used to broken promises, broken relationships, broken dreams, and mistrust. I was broken by words spoken over my life that cut me deep as a knife. I was crying out to my Savior that could only help me whenever I was in need. I would always put God to the test of who he was because I had no example of what he looked like in my life. I would say things like *if you were real, then why this and that*, then all of a sudden he would answer and make me laugh. What a beautiful relationship between my Heavenly Father and me, his daughter.

He keeps his words to me even to this very day. I know that his Jesus is the only way. He is the truth and the light; my soul can now take delight.

At one time in my life, I was in a dark place, but I was bought by his love and amazing Grace. Christ gave up his spirit just for me a long time ago way back on Calvary. Beaten and bruised for all my sins so that I can live.

I see the eagle as it soars in the sky, wondering how the time has flown by. As a child, I can remember the small still voice so vividly inside my head, hearing the very word that God said. You will preach the word. What do I know? That is so absurd. Hey, I was six or eight. Who, what, when, where and how was I going to tell people about someone who I barely knew. I asked questions. I challenged those that said they lived for Christ even then because what they spoke was not of God. When they were willing and still committing sin. Even then I didn't know that the enemy didn't like the skin I was in. Put away just like John the Baptist in a prison to think that Satan himself had won the battle. Sadly mistaken, I read the final chapter.

I glorify Christ the prince of peace (Selah). I bless him with my lips, the fruit of his Word brings forth life. As a young girl, I was never made to fit in. I was the wrong piece for that puzzle. I tried to fit, but I kept popping up. I never saw myself the way God saw me.

I thought I was everything that others told me I was. I talked too much. I asked too many questions for my own good. Most of the time, I was misunderstood. I was different and unique. That was the way God made me. The plans for my life were for good and not evil. Sometimes in that plan, the enemy saw a way to get me off track, by not having others to pray for me.

They figured locking me up would be the best thing. Quiet, I would be about secret things that happened to me, but God knew and his love always carried me through.

Depression, oppression, and stressing about the many things in life, thinking it was an easy way out for me. That was how much I was being controlled by the enemy. He used many people that were close to me to cause me pain. Here I am now destined to reign with my King in Glory. From here on out I will tell my story. The story that He desires to be told.

The word says they will overcome by their testimonies. This is true, if it weren't I'd be lying to you. I ran away from people my entire life. Confused, frustrated, and self-hated, all I ever found was chaos and strife. Never really knew what love was. I kept drifting more into darkness because of the pain in my heart. Until one day the Lord showed me the work of his hand, and that I was a part of his **MASTERPLAN!**

I Write As My Heart Sings

My inner soul dances to the beat of your drums
A choir humming in tune as
I have a bright vision of you,
I smell the floating midst of your sweet fragrance perfume
that lingers in the air
You came to my rescue when I was in despair.
Your hand you extend, I gladly accept
for you have lightened my every footstep.
You cultivated my plans and my ways
So that I can have better days.
Love keeps me singing,
Love keeps me smiling
I'm thankful that I'm no longer on a desert island.
Yah, you are the one that watered my dry places,
and plowed the reins of those broken and empty spaces.
You are the Potter and I am the clay,
I welcome you, Yah, to have your perfect way.
Sewing up the torn parts that somehow
had become tattered on my heart,
You removed the ugly ink stains and filled it with
joy and sunshine and shielded it from the rain
I am no longer bound by ungodly soul-ties,
Understanding now how much you truly love me
makes my heart sing.
It sings at the ringing of your bells summoning me
To a banquet just for two,
Oh, my Lord how much I love you.
Adorned in the latest fashion,
your righteousness, beauty, and glory
I am waiting for you to tell me about my story
the one you are rewriting with a sweet ending
I wish I could watch while you are penning.

I can sit for hours in your presence,
engulfed in this essence
As I hear the sound of trees sway in the wind,
I stand, I twirl and I spin.
Just for you my love is so true because of all that you have done,
by the sacrifice of your only beloved son.
Yes! It's true at one time or another I was a slave to sin,
but you stepped in, unlocked my chains, and rebuked,
All of Satan's spells.
I am no longer walking as the living dead,
only because of the blood Yeshua shed.
You spoke and said live!
My dry bones are alive,
as you called my name,
Dead, I no longer remain.
For your ways are true,
That is why I delight myself in You.

No More! No More!

For the last time I cried my last tear
Totally unaware what to make of these feelings I can't compare.
My eyes swollen, God you have my heart that was once broken
My love, my worship, and my praise is my token
I melt at your words that are so soft spoken.
No more, No more!
I cry, and as my flesh begins to die
I die to what rises above the knowledge of you
I die so that I can follow you.
See, your love is sweet as honey and
Your Grace is smooth as nectar
That is dripping steadily from your vine,
Truth you are, and I shall remain connected,
No longer feeling rejected or naked.
No more, No more!
I scream because your peace takes over me, it surpasses my
understanding
The joy of your strength lifts me up whenever I want to quit
You whisper to me I can handle it.
I stand to face what lies before me,
Just blessings of what you have in store for me.
Good and not of evil, you see how much
Your Divine love has captured me
Rescued me from a life of crime
Right in the nick of time.
You took the rap for me
Your sentence was life, so you gave up yours for me,
No questions asked; you did what you had to do
This is why I love you.
You pled guilty on the count of me,
As they read off my charges
You stayed quiet

In return for what you did on Calvary I give my life to thee. I
bless you for all **ETERNITY**
Heaven is my Home,
When I arrive there I'll never be alone.
No more, No more!
I smile because You bring happiness to
Once a bitter soul
No more, No more!
It's no longer frozen by the cold.
Your wings cascades all around me
They lift me up when I am down
I run to you when I am in fear
As you collect every one of my tears.
One by one in a jar they go
No more, No more!
Lord, you eased my pain,
You covered and protected me from the rain.
I yell, I still have more to tell
About how you have been there to see me through,
I have to tell everyone how much I love you!

Crying Through God's Eyes

It's okay to feel down, but rest assured that I will carry you
There is nothing that I don't see when it comes to you
I am here for you because I love you.
No matter how the story plays out
I am in control.
My tears are filtering through you so let them fall
One by one the streams of my love
Shall spill from your eyes that I see through.
You are my daughter, and I can see your hurt
I want to touch that very place, that's wounded
I want to mend it if your will let me.
Nothing that you have done can change my vision of you
I made no mistakes in how I created you.
Daughter, you are somebody to me
I knew you before the beginning of time,
The clock that I go by is mine.
Time after time, I cry when
I see you cry in your heart,
I see you even when others don't see you.
Although you are broken right now,
I am the Master carpenter
I am the Master builder
I am the Redeemer too
The only one that can deliver you.
The one that can heal, fix, and repair all that's broken
with a few words that are spoken.
I'm causing you to revisit what has been hidden
I'm causing you to feel what you had grown numb to
In the midst of frustration I'm bringing you revelation .
I'm shifting the time that was stolen from you
My tears flow freely from my eyes to yours
You don't suffer in silence, because I am within you.
I wave my banner over you and the winds of peace
Anger is mine, not for you, my child.
Clearly I am revealing what is hidden even now

My tears of peace
My tears of joy
My tears of sorrow
My tears of love
My tears of grace
My tears of understanding
My tears of happiness
My tears of safety.

Two Into One

This isn't some deep mathematical equation. Being taken from the rib of man was all a part of the Master's plan. Bone of his bone, flesh of his flesh, to love woman as Christ loves his bride, that one day this body will die and back to the earth it goes.

A woman loves deep within her soul, she longs for the love that will keep her safe, warm, and secure, not worried or distressed about the source of her comfort. She knows she was placed here for man, not him for her.

The two intertwine minds, bodies, and souls. It is a beautiful love story waiting to be told. Reminds me of the story about Ruth, selected by God to reign with her King as his Queen. Even then man knew his place. His authority and dominion he walked in. She sat at his side and bathed him in prayer. Often broken, a woman like Leah who wanted to be loved, but accepted what was given. Her reward was great. She's responsible for many of the tribe of Israel.

Man knew how to lead a Kingdom of people. Just as Moses fought wars and worshiped liked David, he had dreams and visions like Daniel, John, and Ezekiel. He loved like Peter, whom God loved.

The wife prayed until it was so deep that the sound of her voice was weak. She became Hannah, crying out in pain for God to move by his power and to remember her name. Even then women became a catalyst to bring life into the earth, the carrier of the word as Mary did. About to be put away by her soon to be mate, God sent an angel to reveal to Joseph of the journey they must travel.

God ordained marriage, the vow, and the covenant not to be broken and to become one, instead of two, which is all from Genesis to Revelations. Marriage is between man, woman, and God. A bond not easily broken. The token is a ring, the sign that binds them together as their souls intertwine.

Lukewarm

I have a question.
Are you willing to die? Are you willing to die to sin, to this
wicked world we live in? Have you counted the cost? If not, you
are eternally lost. We say we want God, but because of the
hardness and darkness of our hearts, we will cause many not to
see God. We walk around pretending that things are okay, when
we could lose our very lives today. All because we still think we
have time to play Russian Roulette.

The life that Yeshua gave, we no longer have to be a slave to the
sinful things that we're in. The wages of sin is death. That is a
heavy price to pay, when Yeshua is the only way the truth, and
light. Why keep cheating yourself out of eternal life to be playing
with the enemy's devices.

See from where I sit, the enemy doesn't care about you or me, he
wants to us to stay bound so we can live with him, in hell, which
can become reality. We have to stop allowing the flesh to win
because of sin. God turned his back on his son because he
became sin, who was sinless, to give us his best, so that we can
live in paradise and enjoy the finer things in Christ. So that we
can have sweet rest.

Many loved the talk of tradition not even really sought out to see
why they were commissioned in the first place. We learned how
to do this and that, but we've never really learned how to carry
our own cross and follow him, but instead we allow our spirit
man to grow dim. No strength to fight the wiles of the enemy,
because we drank from the cup of our archenemy, which he was
humiliated for us in the public, brutally.

Please, God, deny the flesh so that you can have eternal rest.

Turn from sin, don't keep allowing the enemy to win, all because
of you are willing to willfully sin. What if you lost your life
today, do you know right now what will be your final resting
place? Will it be in heaven, among the angels, with God who sits
on the throne and Jesus who sits at his right hand. Is it worth to
risk it all to allow your flesh to glory in? We must be hot or cold.
Didn't you read that in God's word?

Lukewarm is not it because those are not the pieces to this
puzzle, that just won't fit in. The Bible gives us a road map to
live just as Christ did, no reason to die before our time just to
live it up on cheap and tasteless wine. We run to what is wicked,
accepting that first class/one-way ticket, on the train to hell. The
enemy loves to play games with our lives.

He never plays fair. Are you willing to place your bet? See, the
enemy knows as long as you play Russian Roulette you are
going to take that bullet that releases from that chamber. Here are
the games that he loves to play. Hide and go seek, but when he
finds you, it's always for keeps.
He seeks out. He's a wolf in sheep's clothing.

Can you see how he tries to deceive? Yes, I am mad at the
enemy. Because he is a liar, cheater, and a killer. He's two-faced.
He'll give you this picture and make it seem so real. Only to
cause you to lose sight of God's purpose for your life.
Then there it goes, you letting down the walls for a cheap thrill,
then he runs and tells the Master what you did. That's for real.
He doesn't care to play fair. Many are called, but few are chosen.
Do not be the pun or the token in his game of chess.

The enemy deals you a hand, a full house. All the time he is
pretending he has a bad hand. Then you play your cards: Ace,
King, and Queens and even a Jack or two,
but little did you know he has both Jokers.
Now the joke is on you, as he tightens his ropes.

102

Christ said his burdens are light and his yoke is easy. Christ gave himself up to death, so that we could receive wealth and an inheritance. What would you gain if you chose the enemy and death? What would be your penalty? Is it worth it to live a lie and die in sin all because of your desires overrule Holy Spirit? Because you've become your own god, and followed the deceit within your heart. I ask you this day to choose to live a life of love, so you can dwell with Christ and be his bride and his wife.

Do not deny God's riches, his might, or glory. Please don't allow the enemy to tell this story. His fate has already been sealed, he doesn't get another chance. See, he was placed on display as he fell from heaven like lightning to burn for all eternity in the bottomless pit with his army and overpowering stench of sulfur. Is it really worth it to be
Lukewarm?

Eternity

I need to tell you about a man that gave up his life, so that one you and I could live in paradise. He created himself a body to come and rescue us from sin; he overcame the cross, death and rose again. Justice was so unfair that he endured our faults. His back was ripped opened and torn form his bones, so that one-day heaven would be our home.

We turn our backs and follow temptation, lies, and lust. In other words, we never lean on God whom we should really trust. He spoke throughout His Word that he would die and rise again on the third day; little did we know that he came to give life in an abundant way.

Loved by few, and hated by many, Even for them he gave up plenty. He prayed until he gave up his spirit, and his Father turned his face from him so that he could see death. He is King of the Jews, they made him a crown, ripped his robe, in the world his love story oftentimes goes untold. A man so pure and righteous became guilty and judged by Pilate Pontius. He was innocent I say, even now people will rather die, than to live a holy way.

Ashamed for others to know that they serve God that will do anything but fail, that is why He sent his son to take the nails. He taught those that followed after him, Yeshua is righteous. He loved all, and hated sin. That is why his love always wins. His love covers a multitude, even though we can sometimes be rude, Never wanting to die to our flesh, we would rather die in our mess. Thinking we have plenty of time. How silly can that be when Yeshua came to set the captives free.

No longer bound by the enemy of this world, we have been given a way of escape. We can't enter into the pearly gates, if we keep on our path of sin, because then death will always win. Somewhere down the line we haven't counted up the cost, if we did, there is great wealth that we would have lost.

Ornitha Danielle

Time Has Come...

Prophetic poetic flow
This is the first time I am writing this straight from the
Holy Spirit!

Time Has Come...
Yet once again
I've knocked on the doors of your heart
I breathe my breath upon your soul,
my child and my love has not grown cold
For I wait until you open up your heart and let me in.
Remember, I am the only that can forgive all your sins.

Time Has Come...
Yet once again, you are my blood dipped pen
You are my letter, I speak to you with the stroke of each letter
that forms, in your thoughts, transferred to pen, to paper that
comes to comfort, correct and warn,
I am mending **ALL** that's broken and torn
Don't leave now, please stay a little while
There's much more I need to share with you, my beloved child
See it wasn't some weird coincidence
that you're reading this poem

Time Has Come...
Yet once again, I am a trusted friend!
Love isn't just a four-letter word,
I explained, said, and expressed it in my Holy Word.
Come one, come all, I'm trying to tear down your built up walls
I am your strong tower, your safety net, and the glory shall
gracefully enlighten the depths of your soul,
as I said before, my love doesn't grow cold.
For you I fight to the end, see the enemy is not a trusted friend,
he's been a liar, I have created a place for him.

It's a place that has unquenchable **FIRE**!
Nothing you've done is so bad, to keep you from me,
because I paid your debt back on Calvary.
You will be with me in Paradise, a place with many luxuries.
A place that is not of here,
beyond what your mind could ever dream
Know that my place is supreme.
With my **LOVE**, pearly gates, joy, peace, crowns, and robes.
Yes, even the streets are gold.
It's true what you've been told,
about the things that you've heard, read and seen
in the midst of your dreams.
Brighter days are not far off.
You see me waving my hand in the distance.
When you talk to me, you truly have my undivided attention.
I respond within an instant
I move heaven and earth, oceans, seas, mountains, big and small
streams; to provide just what you need and what you've asked
Be patient my child something's do take a while.

Time Has Come...

Yet once again, I control it – **TIME**
I want to mend all of the broken parts
Within your heart, mind and soul,
As I have said before, my love for you never grows cold.
My loving arms await, come my child, and cast your cares upon
me, because I care for you.
What concerns you, concerns me too!
I have proven myself many times through and through.
Come my son, come my daughter, let me love you
Let me shower you with my love and **I AM**.
I landed upon my son, as a white heavenly dove.
Radiating my glory as I am telling this story
Spring, Summer, Fall and Winter
It doesn't matter what season it is
I move in ways yet so unknown.

Ornitha Danielle

Even when you think you are alone, **REMEMBER**
I am the one who sits upon the throne
Nothing passes my eyes or my ears,
Please, my child, let me take away all of your
frustration and fears.
As you are deep in thought,
wondering about the essence of me, come closer and see.
Drink from my cup, it has the power to quench that thirst.
Eat from my table.
Time Has Come...
yet once again
You are my beloved, my precious jewel,
and my love for you runs deep, as you drift off to sleep.
No need to count sheep,
Rest I will give thee, **Time Has Come...**
yet once again,
I love you, just abide in me.

Winter Thoughts

As I meditate upon the things of God, ice, rain, sleet, howling of the winds blowing, and the trees crashing against the roof, I can't help but wonder at the glory that's in the midst. Oh, the things that we sometimes take for granted.

I listen to every single crystal of ice, sounding like the tingling of
glass being tapped so lightly on its rim.
The thrusting of the wind,
it's in the earth's atmosphere as we are being shifted
in the next dimension of the hemisphere.
As time travels, only God controls,
Thinking about the Kingdom, and priestly robes.
The crown of jewels that will adorn one's head,
we are joint heirs all because of the blood Christ shed.
An invitation that awaits, for one to open, how amazing that I
was invited to dine with the King. A feast prepared by his hand.
Of all the finest things,
It is hard not to imagine the delicacies, the fine linens, fancier
than I hoped for, nothing like it have I ever seen.
Truly, it has exceeded far beyond my childish dreams.
The things we have seen and are led to believe in the movies, of
Cinderella, and Snow White the fairytale of happily ever after!
It is the wedding that has been talked about for many years, this
can be reality not some fantasy. We are going to reign with the
one who sits on the throne; because Heaven is where we belong.
However, until then, I will just continue to listen to the rustling
of the wind and thanking God that he calls me his friend.

ABOUT ORNITHA DANIELLE

Ornitha Danielle is the proud mother of three children, grandmother of one and wife to Rodney 'Lee' Taylor who is a professional freelance photographer. She now resides in Somerville, Tennessee, where she writes full-time, and pursuing her dreams as a Christian Author, teacher (*SCRIBE*), Blogger, Editor-in-Chief of So Fyh Magazine Online, Poet, Educator, Minister, Prophetic Praise Worshipper, Inspirational and Motivational Speaker.

In her former career, she was a professional hairstylist and makeup artist, which allowed her to be chic, unique, edgy, and very creative.

With the many things that God has placed in her hands, she is able to move freely in Him. Ornitha Danielle is truly God's Scribal Prophet. She has reached beyond the surface, extended her eagle wings, soared further than the clouds and became an educator in her field of expertise. She taught at several beauty schools in the Memphis area. She later became a salon owner of *Perfection of Beauty*. After working many years as a Master Stylist for a well-known franchise, she decided to return to school.

After graduating from Community College, it opened a very different perspective on one of her many loves, which happened to be the love of writing. Her grasp of the love for words, and freedom of written expression, her craft of creative writing has allowed this novelist to venture into a new marketplace and create that path for her unique style of writing.

She is a fulltime freelance journalist for many publications, one being the Tri-State Defender Newspaper in Memphis, Tennessee among many other publications including her own online magazine, So Fyh Magazine Online. She is an online radio personality for "Let's Talk Literary with Ornitha Danielle," and a media journalist for Black Butterfly Media TV. She is National Media Director for Voices of Christ Literary International Ministries and the visionary of Souls Ignited International Ministries.

This new area in her life as a career businesswoman and ministry in motion has found its home in Literary Ministry. Ornitha Danielle is currently working on her Bachelor of Science degree in Media Communications, and working on many other projects as well as penning her next of many novels.